Preface

This is a story about a man who wanted to spend more time with his children. To do it, he had to learn how to control his finances rather than have his finances control him. Whatever your reason is for reading this story, may it give you the information you need to realize your dreams.

Acknowledgements

This book came about with the help of a large team. I would like to express immense thanks to my friends and family for their continual support. Thank you Eileen, my wife, for your continual love and patience. Thank you to Eric and Jean-Luc, my two sons, for your constant sources of energy and inspiration. I'd also like to express gratitude to my parents, and to my wife's parents, for their generous guidance in my growth.

Special thanks go to the advance readers who gave their input on how to make the book better: Wayne Barclay, John Fuoco, Nathalie Amyotte, Barry McMahon, Peggy McColl, Bob Urichuk, Denis Fortin, and Tom Froggatt.

You need to take a lot of shots on the net before you can figure out how to score. Thank you ToastMasters, especially my home club of Uplands Wingtalkers, for the willingness to hear my ideas in their infancy, and to give me suggestions on how those ideas can best be expressed to help others. Thanks as well to the Ottawa chapter of CAPS (Canadian Association of Public Speakers), and all its members for their education and encouragement.

Any game is easier to play when you enjoy it. Many thanks are due to Darlene Cherry. She was instrumental in coaching me towards my passion, and in helping me to develop the confidence to proceed in that direction. As well, I would like to express my gratitude to Wayne Barclay, Peggy McColl, James Maduk and Bob Urichuk for being extremely helpful in giving me the knowledge I needed to move forward.

The publishing of this book had its own wet tennis balls. Fortunately, I was able to get around, over and through obstacles with good players on my side. Wendy O'Keefe and Gail Baird helped me immeasurably with the publishing plan. Janet Shorten did a fantastic editing job, and Fernando Martinez has done wonders with the cover design. Michelle Valberg has done an excellent job with her cover photos, and Marie Tappin has laid out the insides beautifully. Thank you all so much!

I would be remiss not to mention my late great uncle, Don Munro. He invented the first table top hockey game decades ago. Thank you Uncle Don for allowing generations of children to enjoy hockey in their own home, when the weather was too poor to participate in the greatest sport of them all — street hockey.

Table of Contents

Warm Up

Everyone Loves Street Hockey

It was Saturday, and Pete Smith was feeling frustrated. For the third time in four months, he'd had to spend an extra day at the office. Pete should have been watching his son play hockey at the local arena. Instead, he was watching the photocopier print copies of his latest report.

Pete was almost forty, and burning both ends of the candle just to make ends meet. He had recently been promoted, but still he didn't feel as if he was doing well enough. Even though his career and salary had improved, he couldn't see the light at the end of the tunnel. His raise was barely enough to meet his expenses, and there were hardly any savings to fall back on.

So the guilt of missing his son's game was bearable, Pete thought to himself. Pete's father had never missed one of his games, but times were different when Pete was a child.

Pete grabbed the reports and headed to his office. As he walked towards the filing cabinet, he caught a glimpse of some neighborhood children out the window. They were playing street hockey in the distance. It looked as though one of the children had just got a new net, and his father was helping him put it together.

Pete sat down in his chair. He began reminiscing about how he had fallen in love with street hockey around the time that he got his first net. It was Christmas Day in 1970. He was seven years old, and it was the prettiest sight in the world – a brand new street hockey net, sitting in front of the fireplace, shining brightly. The webbing on the net was whiter than the snow falling gently outside his suburban Montreal home. Although there were three hockey sticks resting against the net, Pete ran to the net and claimed it as his own.

Pete had been arranging street hockey games every day after school since Hallowe'en. He always got the other equipment ready, and always tried to make sure the teams were fair. So his brothers didn't mind that he wanted to be in charge of the net.

Pete continued to play street hockey for years. In September of 1972, he had a major "hockey moment." The team of Canadian players representing almost every NHL team was playing an eight-game series against the U.S.S.R., and after the seventh game the series was tied. The eighth and deciding game was being held in the U.S.S.R., and Pete pleaded with his mother to call in sick so he could stay home and watch this pivotal game. His mother would have nothing to do with his plan.

Pete's discouragement soon turned to joy when he found out the school was broadcasting the game on television sets in several of the rooms. He was watching when, with less than a minute left, Paul Henderson scored the biggest goal to date in international play, to let the Canadians win. Pete was so excited, he did something he had never done before, and something he would never do for another thirty years – he hugged another boy. Pete was very inspired by that goal; he would often look back on it later when he needed motivation.

Pete played many forms of hockey. He played in the school gym with plastic sticks and a plastic puck. He played in organized ice hockey leagues, both indoor and outdoor. The outdoor games were special for Pete. On Saturday afternoons, the parents would band together between periods and shovel off the snow when it got too deep to play. When the games were played at night, Pete's toes would freeze and then go numb and then burn while they returned to their natural state once he returned home.

As more arenas were built, and Pete's skills improved, Pete played more indoor games, but he never gave up his love for street hockey. He liked the non-ideal weather conditions of playing in the street, and he loved the spontaneity of getting together with friends. Pete had an advantage outside because he was a gritty competitor. While snow and wind would throw others off their game, Pete would welcome the weather challenges. He didn't feel challenged in school. He was learning at a good pace, and consistently getting good marks. When he did run into trouble, he'd compare the problem at hand to street hockey, and then figure it out.

Pete was particularly good at math. This grew into a strong desire to learn statistics – especially hockey statistics. To challenge himself, Pete tried to memorize the statistics from the back of every hockey card that either he or his brothers owned.

Pete moved several times between Montreal and Ottawa. Sure enough, his best way of meeting new friends was to drag his net out on the street, and then ask the neighborhood children for a game.

By the time Pete graduated from high school, he wasn't sure what he wanted to do. Because he was good in math, his school's guidance counselor suggested that he follow in his father's footsteps and take engineering. In the fall of 1981, Pete began his studies in Electrical Engineering at the University of Waterloo.

Pete lived in residence, and was pleased to discover that many of the other students living on his male-only floor enjoyed playing hockey. After the first semester's mid-terms, Pete was happy to find out about a sport called cage hockey. This game involved playing ball hockey in a common room, with metal bars on the windows so the ball wouldn't break them. The games were organized spontaneously, and it was a great change from the everyday grind which Pete had not developed much passion for.

Three of Pete's floormates – Steve, Eric and Jean-Luc – had schedules that coincided well with Pete's. They played 2-on-2 games twice a week, and soon were challenging others in a residence-wide league. The following year, Pete was not lucky enough to get back into residence. Steve decided to move off-campus as well, and the "cage hockey gang" was no longer together.

Pete graduated with good marks, and was able to find a good job. After working his way up to a team leader position, he decided to take a chance on a fairly new technology company. He figured the technology was much more modern, and his chances for advancement were also much better.

Soon Pete met a woman that he couldn't live without. He married Jenny, and not long afterwards they had two children, both boys. He promised each of them that he would teach them the joys of street hockey, and play with them whenever he could.

When Pete was promoted to senior manager, he moved his family to a middle-class neighborhood in the south end of Ottawa. For Hallowe'en, Pete visited his new neighborhood with his children. He hadn't gotten out much since his recent move, so he welcomed the opportunity to meet the neighbors. Much to Pete's surprise, one of his old cage hockey friends, Steve Murphy, lived a few houses down. As they caught up on old times, Pete discovered that Steve had not fared as well in his career as Pete had. Steve had taken an extra year to graduate, and then he had never been able to move into a management position. Two years earlier, Steve had left his job at the local telephone company, and was still in transition. Pete knew far too many engineers in this position.

Winter descended in Ottawa. As the days grew shorter, so did Pete's temper. His drive to work was now getting very long, as the poor weather conditions caused drivers to slow down. One evening, Pete was frazzled when he came home late for supper.

"What's wrong?" Jenny asked.

"Those darn Murphys are playing street hockey and they just missed my rearview mirror with their tennis ball," Pete replied.

"Are they still out there?" Jenny looked towards the window, oblivious to Pete's near clash. "They've been playing since 3 o'clock this afternoon."

"I just don't get how Steve can stay home and play street hockey for three hours with his kids, while I'm stuck working late on yet another overdue project that I had no control over," Pete said despondently.

Jenny offered, "Maybe you should talk to him about it. He hasn't worked since he got laid off, yet he's still living in this up-scale neighborhood."

On the following Saturday, Pete's son, Nicolas, would be playing against Steve's son, Tom. Pete decided he'd take the opportunity to approach Steve then.

Unfortunately, Pete couldn't make the game. With his project running late, he had to go into the office to catch up. While Terry took it in stride, Jenny was less impressed. "Come on, Pete! It seems like every month, you're spending another weekend at the office. It's not fair to Terry or to me!"

Pete countered, "I don't like it any more than you do. I have no control over these projects. I'm always done my part on time, but somebody else always comes in late. And it always seems to be the most important person that's late."

So here he was, stuck in the office instead of watching his son play hockey. Meanwhile, Steve was out playing street hockey for three hours a day with his kids. What weighed more on Pete's brain was that street hockey used to be the love of his life – now, it was just a nuisance.

Although he'd missed his son's hockey game, he decided he still had to get hold of Steve. He had to find out what Steve's secret was. Although he didn't see how Steve could be in a better position than he was, he decided then and there that he *had* to find out how someone his age could afford to play street hockey all afternoon with his kids.

"Steve?" Pete asked, when he finally dialed Steve's number. "Can I take you out for a beer tonight and watch the Senators mop up the floor with the Maple Leafs?"

"I'm glad you called," Steve responded. "Unfortunately, we were just heading to the Corel Centre to watch the game. How about Tuesday night after the kids are asleep?" Pete invited him over to his house, and then headed home, anxiously awaiting the Tuesday meeting.

What seemed like an eternity finally ended with Steve ringing the bell at 8:55. Jenny let him in, and they all sat down in the family room.

"We haven't spoken in a while," Steve offered.

Pete got right to the point. "Steve, I don't know how you do it! You've been laid off for two years, and we've been wondering when you were going to sell your house. Your wife doesn't work outside the home, and yet you've just bought a new car (although it's not as nice as my Lexus). How do you do it?"

Steve started shaking his head. "I was never laid off. I was offered incentives to leave, so I took them."

"Yeah, whatever, Steve," Pete stated. "So where is your money coming from?"

Steve responded, "I have several income-producing assets. Where does your money come from?"

Pete replied proudly, "I've just been promoted to Senior Manager! I got quite a nice raise too!"

"Congratulations, Pete! I'm glad to hear you're doing well," Steve said.

Pete looked down at his hands. Even though his career and salary had improved, his raise was barely enough to meet his expenses. And he knew Jenny was already planning on "celebrating" the new money with a nice trip at Spring Break.

Pete suddenly remembered why he was there. He looked up at his old friend and asked, "What do you mean by income-producing assets?"

Steve responded with a long-winded account of financial terms. When he realized Pete had tuned out, he stopped. "Pete? You've got the same expression on your face as I did when I spoke to my Uncle Ken for the first time about controlling my money. He taught me a lot about finances – how to control your spending, how to get your money working for you and how to increase your finances. But it didn't make sense for a long time until I was able to relate it to something I could understand."

"Hockey?" Pete asked.

"Exactly!" Steve affirmed.

Jenny left the room just then, and Steve looked Pete in the eye. "What's your biggest challenge these days?"

Pete took a deep breath and sighed. "My biggest challenge is that I have no control over my life! It doesn't matter how much money I make; it's never enough. I don't have time to do the things I want to do because all my non-work time (which is disappearing yearly) is spent lugging the kids around to hockey games, swimming classes and piano lessons."

"Wow," Steve interjected.

Pete continued, "My boss doesn't think I work hard enough, and my wife doesn't think I'm at home enough. The truth is, I'm too busy making a living to . . ."

Steve completed the sentence. "You're too busy making a living to make a life."

"Exactly," Pete responded, exasperated. Jenny came back and set down a few bowls of nuts and chips. She rubbed Pete's back, in an effort to comfort him.

"How can I help?" Steve asked solemnly.

Pete looked up and said, "I want to know your secret! I want to know how you can live in the same kind of house as I have, without a job. I want to know how I did so much better in school than you, and then got a better-paying job than you, and yet still struggle to make ends meet, while you play street hockey with your kids."

Steve took a sip of his beer. "It all started when I went to register for my first year of university. It was the summer of '81. The post office was on strike . . . again."

Jenny joked, "No wonder the Internet became so popular so quickly."

The mood became much lighter. Pete was settling back, and Steve continued to reminisce, "My parents drove me down to Waterloo to sign up. When we got there, we stopped at a house in Kitchener. Apparently, we were visiting my Uncle Ken. Up to this point, I didn't even know I had an Uncle Ken. My mother told me on the drive home that he was the black sheep of the family. Anyway, he gave me his phone number and told me to call him. I gave a polite okay, with no real intention of ever seeing this stranger again, especially after my mother's warnings.

"But after school started, I needed a ride one weekend and phoned Uncle Ken to see if he could help me out. He offered to take me out for supper and we started talking.

"It started off pretty rough," Steve continued. "He was asking me some personal things that even my parents never spoke to me about."

"This is getting interesting," Jenny joked.

"I wish," Steve answered. " Actually, the questions he was asking me were about money . . . and dreams . . . and my future. I guess my parents had probably tried to talk to me about these things, but teenagers just think they're being lectured to. So I tuned out my parents. But Uncle Ken also had a different perspective. Whereas my Mom was trying to get me to focus on being safe and following the pack, my Uncle Ken tried to get me to focus on being idealistic and following my dreams."

"Which is why you failed second year?" Pete broke in jokingly, although Jenny was clearly not amused.

Steve remarked dryly, "I actually failed second year due to bad plumbing and faulty wiring, but that's another story. When Uncle Ken pushed me to state what I really wanted to do with my life, I blurted out, of all things, 'I just want to play street hockey. I went into Engineering because everyone thought I should, but the only joy in my life is playing street hockey. If I could, I'd play street hockey three hours a day, and everything else would fit into that schedule.' Although I feared ridicule from this rarely seen uncle, he just leaned over and said to me, 'So . . . what's stopping you?' 'Well, for one thing,' I shot back, 'you can't make money playing street hockey!'"

"You told him!" Pete intervened.

"The funny thing is," Steve continued, "he just laughed at that comment. Then he laughed some more."

"That must have been hard on you," Jenny said in a supporting voice.

"It might have been, Jenny," Steve continued, "but then he got a glint in his eye. He looked at me and said, 'You might not be able to make money playing street hockey, but what if you could set up methods of making enough money that you could play street hockey as often as you wish?'

"That sounded great but of course my next question was, How? Uncle Ken responded, 'You told me that Wayne Gretzky is set to make one million dollars over the next twenty years. What if you were to have one million dollars in your pocket in twenty years' time? Would that be enough?'

"I was intimidated by my Uncle Ken's comments. Little old me having one million dollars in my pocket? Money didn't run in my family. I asked him how that was possible.

"So Uncle Ken made me write down a goal. It took a while to get the right wording, but we came up with this: I, Steve Murphy, have one million dollars in assets on November 1, 2001. Then, he made me commit to saying the goal out loud every day, and then to visualizing myself with one million dollars. Somehow, my Uncle Ken had this idealistic 18-year-old engineering student believing he was worth as much as Wayne Gretzky." Steve grinned. "'If you believe it, you can achieve it,' he always used to say. And he told me that earning money while doing something fun is the goal of most retirees without a pension. When you retire, he told me, you're living off your assets. The sooner you learn how to live off your assets, the better."

"So he taught you a lot?" Jenny asked.

"First, he taught me how to buy real estate with no down payment. When I told my mother I'd bought a house, and was now renting it to other students, she told me to stop meeting with Uncle Ken for supper. I wasn't going to argue with my mother . . . so we started meeting for lunch! I got so addicted to buying these no-money-down deals, I had six of them by the end of first year. They were totaling less than $10 a month profit, and interest rates were 17.5 percent. My mother thought I was justifiably insane, but Uncle Ken told me patience was key in winning at the money game.

"Still, when we started talking about financial planning and creating wealth, I had a really hard time listening. I couldn't relate to most of the terms and, frankly, I found the discussions quite boring. With Uncle Ken's help, I was able to get energetic and enthusiastic about it, though, by relating it to something I could care about . . . street hockey!"

"Now that's a language I can understand," Pete mused.

"By the time I graduated," Steve went on, "the monthly profits on the townhouses had gone up to over

$800 per month. Those six units, I'm glad to report, are now paid off, and worth several hundred thousand dollars.

"To reach my goal of having one million dollars in my pocket, I also had to learn how to save money. Uncle Ken taught me some interesting ideas. Rather than rest on real estate laurels, I also got into investing some of my profits in financial products. I bought mutual funds, and they did very well in the '90s. The good thing about mutual funds was that the money I made was hassle-free. There were no tenants, and no leaky faucets to fix. As well, I was able to get the most out of my job. I became very specialized in what I was doing, and when I left, I was making more money than my manager was!

"Five years ago, I started looking into setting up a business on the side. When I took a voluntary lay-off, I was able to go into the business full time. Now, I work on the business in the morning and at night. This leaves me all afternoon to play street hockey with the kids!"

"Listen," Jenny said. "Pete and I are very intrigued and could obviously learn a lot from your experiences. Would you mind sharing more of them with us next week?"

"One of the most important things my Uncle Ken taught me is that giving is more important than receiving," Steve replied. "Besides, I need more people to play with that are closer to my age. During the day, the only people that can play are over sixty . . . and they all seem to want to play goalie. I would look forward to teaching you everything I've learned over the last twenty years about making financial goals, planning your financial future and creating wealth."

"Is it okay then if I invite my brother and his 18-year-old son along?" Jenny asked. "I know my nephew, in particular, has a lot of questions about his financial future."

Steve nodded. "Please invite them. One of the biggest advantages of creating wealth is to get started early."

Jenny thanked Steve. As she closed the door behind him, she looked at Pete and joked, "Last week, you were calling him a Street Hockey Bum. The truth is, he's a Street Hockey Millionaire."

Practice Session 1
Know What Type of Player You Are

Jenny's brother Mark looked young for a man who had just turned fifty. When he entered with his 18-year-old son Chris, Mark asked Jenny who her friend was. Jenny introduced them to Steve. Mark said, "It's a pleasure to meet you, Steve. You should know Chris is heading off to Boston College on a hockey scholarship in the fall. Is this stuff you're teaching us going to help him in the U.S.?"

Steve replied, "Personal finances are very similar in Canada and the United States, and all over the world, for that matter. As we go on, I'll describe some subtle differences between terms used in the two countries and some differences in tax laws for each of the countries. If Chris ends up in Europe, Australia or South East Asia, he'll still be able to use the information I'll be giving you over the next few weeks. There may be a few differences in the terms and tax laws, but the principles are the same no matter which country you live in.

"Now, let's get started on improving your financial situation. The first thing you need to know is what type of player you are."

"Okay," Chris chipped in, "I'm a goalie." The others looked amused. They knew Steve had something else on his mind.

Steve continued, "I'm going to be teaching you things by using hockey terms. As we go along, you'll realize that success in personal finance is similar to success in hockey. Similar, but not exactly the same. When I say 'What type of player are you?', I mean in terms of the personal finance game."

"What does our playing ability have to do with making money?" Chris asked, looking perplexed.

"Personal finances," Steve continued, "are more than making money. As we get into later lessons, you'll realize that your personal wealth may or may not be closely tied to your income. You will have to make choices about how to make your money. As you make money, you will have to choose what to do with it. You may choose to buy a new car. You may travel. You may save it all for a rainy day. Or you may decide to give all your money to charity. Because everyone has a limited amount of time and money, everyone has to make decisions about what they do with their time and money. That's what I mean by 'what kind of player are you?' I'm really asking where your priorities are. Also, where are your skills and talents? There is no 'one size fits all' plan for succeeding at personal finances."

"Actually," Pete observed, "hockey sweaters that say 'one size fits all' never fit anybody." Everyone chuckled.

"I could tell you everything you need to know to succeed in personal finances, but it would mean nothing if you had no reason to do it," Steve asserted. "Tonight's exercises will help you later on in prioritizing your goals, making game plans, deciding how you're going to spend your time and money, and then setting up your defensive and offensive strategies." As Steve looked around, he noticed everyone's look of surprise. The students had either underestimated how much was involved in financial planning, or they didn't realize how much Steve knew. Either way, Steve decided he'd better simplify things.

He returned to his original subject. "Let's look at what type of players you are in terms of personal finance. I've prepared a few sets of questions for you." He handed out the first questionnaire. "Please take your time filling out your answers."

Mark chipped in, "My answers to these questions aren't going to be the same now as they were when I was Chris's age."

Steve replied, "It's just natural that everyone matures. You may realize talents only when you start activities that let those talents shine. What we want to get at is what you enjoy today. You need to find out where your priorities lie now, and where you choose to spend your time and money. As we get further into these lessons, you'll have a much better idea of how to apply these principles if you give some serious thought to these questions.

"The first thing we need to know is where your strengths and weaknesses are. We need to take a personal inventory so that we can optimize your money-making power. When it comes to making money, the people who are experts usually command the most money. Let's look at where your expertise lies now, and where your interests lie. It may be that you could be making a lot more money doing something other than what you're currently doing. But to become an expert requires commitment, so choose something you'd enjoy pursuing."

Questionnaire #1 Personal Inventory

1. When I was in school, people told me I was good at

_____

_____

_____

_____

2. When I was in school, I really enjoyed

_____

_____

_____

_____

3. When I was in school, my best courses were _____

_____

_____

_____

_____

4. When I was in school, the courses I enjoyed the most were

_____

_____

_____

_____

5. When I finished school, I decided to

_____

_____

because _____

_____

_____

6. On the job, I've been told I'm good at

_____

_____

_____

_____

7. My friends outside work tell me my greatest
   strengths are

_____

_____

_____

_____

8. The thing I enjoy most about my current job is

_____

_____

_____

_____

9. In my spare time, I enjoy

_____

_____

_____

_____

10. My ideal job is

_____

_____

_____

_____

"When you look at your answers to these questions, do you see any patterns? Do you notice how your skills and interests have changed over the years? Do you think your current skills and interests match your current occupation? Do you see a direction that you would like to move your life towards?

"This next set of questions will look at the obstacles you face in making more money. It could be that the main reason you don't make more money is that you don't think you're worth it."

Questionnaire #2 Views About Money

1. Money is _____

2. To my spouse, money means _____

3. To my parents, money was _____

4. Debt is _____

5. Savings are _____

6. Rich people are _____

7. Poor people are _____

8. To be comfortable, I need
   this much money in savings: _____

9. I feel uncomfortable when I
   have savings less than _____

10. Owing people is bad because _____

11. If I were going to owe money
    to anybody, it would be to _____

12. Owing people is good because _____

13. If I needed to save more money,
    I would _____

14. If I needed to earn more money,
    I would _____

15. If my paycheck were cut by
    10 percent, I would sacrifice _____

16. If I could afford it, I'd _____

17. Being wealthy means _____

18. Being successful means _____

19. The most money I'll ever make is _____

20. The most money I'll ever have
    in the bank is _____

Steve gave them time to fill out the questionnaire. Then he went on. "Look at the answers you've written. Do you see any patterns? What good does it serve to believe the things you do? How does it hurt you to have these beliefs?

"We've looked at who you are, and what obstacles you may be facing in reaching your maximum potential. Next, I'm going to take away all the obstacles. I want you to spend some time this week thinking about these answers. You won't be able to answer them in one sitting tonight. So take this third questionnaire home with you."

Questionnaire #3 Where You Want to Go

1. If time and money were no object, what would you
   do? _____
   _____
   _____
   _____
   _____
   _____
   _____

2. If you were guaranteed to succeed, what would you
   do?_____
   _____
   _____
   _____
   _____
   _____
   _____
   _____

3. If a genie could appear and give you any five
   objects you desire, what would you ask the genie
   for? _____
   _____
   _____
   _____
   _____
   _____

4. If, on the other hand, your doctor told you that you had contracted a rare disease that gives you six months of pain-free time to live, followed by a painless death, what would you do in those last six months? _____

_____

_____

_____

_____

_____

_____

5. What events are coming up in the next 5, 10 or 20 years of your life that you need money for?

_____

_____

_____

_____

_____

_____

"This has been a short session. We've looked at where your strengths lie, what your beliefs about money are, and where you want to go with your life. In order for the group of you to improve your financial situation, you're going to have to make changes. Thinking that things are going to change if you keep doing the same things is unreasonable.

"To finish this week, I would like to give you some homework. In addition to filling out the third questionnaire, make a list of all the dreams you have for the future: what you want to have, where you want to go, what you want to become and what you want to do. A dream exists in the imagination. To bring it to reality, we make it into a goal. So write down your goals and bring them with you next week. Then we'll look at how to bring your goals closer to reality."

Pete said, "All I want to be able to do is to enjoy some time with my children. How am I going to find time to do that?"

Jenny comforted him, "Don't worry Pete. Next week, Steve will teach us how to 'score' our goals."

Practice Session 2
Learn to Score Your Goals

Pete welcomed in the other players. "Coach Steve is downstairs waiting for us. Do you guys know what type of players you are?"

Mark replied, "I haven't had time to think much about that stuff since Chris was born. It sure helps my focus to think about how I really want to spend my time and money."

Chris added, "It's going to take me a while to figure this stuff out."

Jenny was sitting down, waiting patiently for the others. Coach Steve saw them coming down the stairs, and then started into his speech.

"I know that self-discovery is a long process and I don't expect any of you to master it in a week. But when you have a firm lock on where you want to go, what you want to have, or even who you want to be, there are certain steps you need to take to reach those goals."

Jenny broke in, "You mean score those goals?"

The men laughed. For someone who didn't understand hockey, Jenny's ability to mix hockey with humor was starting to impress the hockey aficionados.

"That's right," Steve continued. "You need to follow a certain process to 'score' the goals you've set for yourself. There are five steps, and I'll explain each one to you, and then review them at the end.

"The first thing you need to do is make a scorecard of your goals. That is, you have to write them all down, and leave a space beside them to check them off when you've achieved them."

"What does this have to do with financial planning, Steve?" Pete asked.

"Good question, Pete," Steve replied. "Some of your goals will be financial goals. Many of the other things you want to be, have or do will probably impact your financial goals. Let's say, for instance, that Pete has the goal of putting his kids through university or college. That will definitely affect his financial goals. Similarly, if Mark wants to travel more, he's probably going to need more money than if his goal for the year is to spend a lot of time gardening. Most people have trouble with financial planning because the money itself does not excite them enough. They need other plans, or dreams, to keep them on track to score their financial goals. So let's move into the process for scoring our goals, shall we?

"As I said before, the first step is making a scorecard of your goals. List everything you want to be, have or do. Since you thought about this over the last week, it shouldn't take too long. Here's an example of a scorecard I made a few years ago."

Scorecard of Goals

	GOAL	Done
1.	I, Steve Murphy, weigh less than 180 pounds on Dec. 31, 2001, so I have more energy to enjoy the things I want to do.	X
2.	I, Steve Murphy, have a net worth over one million dollars on Nov. 1, 2001, so I can afford to play street hockey with my children after school.	X
3.	I, Steve Murphy, am running my own information marketing business on Sept. 1, 2001, so I can earn a healthy income while arranging my time in whatever fashion I choose.	X
4.	I, Steve Murphy, have a network of contacts, which includes at least two lawyers, two accountants, two financial planners and two bankers on Oct. 15, 2001, so I can have access to reliable legal and financial assistance to run my business and to look after my finances.	X

"To let us practice going through the process for each goal," Steve continued, "I want you to choose the one financial goal that means the most to you right now. Can everyone do that?"

"Sure, Coach," Pete said. "I need to pay off my debts."

"Excellent example," Steve replied. "Now, what date do you want to finish that by?"

"Yesterday!" Jenny joked.

"My goal-setting and achieving procedure isn't that good!" Steve smiled. "What timeframe do you feel comfortable with, Pete?"

Pete thought about it. He hadn't checked his VISA statement recently, but felt comfortable with a six-month timeframe. "I can get out of debt in six months," Pete told the others, somewhat confidently.

Steve probed deeper. "What debt would that include?"

Pete replied, "My VISA debt. It's growing, but I can nip it in the bud in six months or so."

Jenny added, "What about the Sears card and the MasterCard?"

Pete responded, "We don't owe too much on those, do we?"

Steve jumped in, "We're going to get into proper financial habits, including tracking all your debts, assets, income, and so on, next time. For now, let's concentrate on Pete and Jenny paying off their VISA bill in the next six months. Let's look at the scorecard, shall we?" Steve pulled out a blank scorecard, similar to the one he had just shown.

Jenny wrote down at the top of the list, "Try to pay off VISA debt in six months or so."

Steve looked at the goal. "The way the goal is worded can help you to achieve it. Say the goal out loud, and see how it sounds."

Jenny and Pete, although not quite in unison, read the goal aloud. "We can probably do that," Pete added.

Steve asked, "Why do you want to achieve this goal?"

Jenny replied quickly, "So I can start sleeping at night without having to worry about money."

Steve said, "Write that down beside where you wrote the goal. Then repeat the goal, out loud, followed by the reason for needing to do it."

As Pete and Jenny read the goal and the reason aloud, they realized the wording of the goal was fairly weak. "We need to make that goal sound more important," Jenny added, "so I can actually sleep better at night."

"You beat me to the punch," Steve replied. "The goal should be worded confidently, and as if you've already achieved it. This will help immensely later when you're visualizing the goals. The best way to write the goal is: We, Pete and Jenny Smith, have no balance on our VISA card on September 1, 2003, so we can sleep at night."

Pete gasped, "That would be fantastic! The thing is, I've been trying to do this for the last several years. How am I going to succeed this time?"

Steve smiled, "That's the perfect introduction to the second step of the process, namely: Make a game plan to score your goal." Again, Steve took out a piece of paper with a hockey rink in the background.

"Another hockey rink?" Jenny wondered.

"Jenny, this is how coaches show their players how to score goals in hockey," Steve replied. "With a layout of the rink, they'll position all the players so the puck can move up the ice. As the puck is passed from player to player, the setup is made for one player to shoot the puck and. . ."

"Score the goal!" Chris finished.

"Scoring financial goals requires similar planning and forethought," Steve continued. "Let's say your VISA bill is $900. To pay it off in six months, one way would be to pay ... let's see ... $157.75 per month."

Chris intervened, "That would be more than $900, Steve. Shouldn't it be $150 per month?"

Steve responded, "The VISA balance which is unpaid will continue to accrue interest. So the answer is no, we can't just divide the balance by six. That is a common mistake, though, and I'm glad you've pointed that out. Do we all see why debt is such a bad thing?

"If we look at our game plan, a good first step is to calculate monthly payments to pay off the debt. Once we know how much we need per month, what should we do?" Steve looked around at the faces of the gang.

Jenny responded, "Figure out ways to save that much," while Pete was simultaneously responding with "Determine how to make the extra money."

The others laughed. Steve said, "Very good! Both ideas would work well together. For our sample game plan, let's put them down as separate steps towards reaching our goals, with passes between so we can move closer to the goal. Looking at our example, after we've done our research, it's time to decide and implement our methods to reach that balance. You'll probably have to review and modify as the months go by, so let's add that as the last step. Our sample game plan, then, to help Pete and Jenny meet their goal of paying off their debt in six months, would be:

Game Plan to Score Your Goal

*We, Pete and Jenny Smith, have no balance on
our VISA card on September 1, 2003,
so we can sleep at night.*

6. Review plans and modify as required

5. Commit to, and implement, new savings and/or
earning plan.

4. Decide which methods make the most sense.

3. Research methods to earn more money.

2. Research methods to save more money.

1. Determine monthly payment to reach goal.

Mark interrupted, "You know Steve, I had a similar problem six years ago. I had a few credit card bills I just couldn't seem to pay off. I spoke with someone at my bank, and they offered me a consolidation loan. They gave me a two-year loan to pay off all my credit cards at a reduced interest rate. While some of the credit cards had interest rates of 18.5 percent, others had huge rates of 28.5 percent. My consolidation loan was a bargain at 13 percent."

Steve smiled, "Thanks for that story, Mark. It demonstrates the third step of the goal-scoring process: Get a good team behind you. Your example shows the power of teamwork in two different ways. The first is that your banker was part of your team in helping you pay down your debt. He gave you some great advice, and then helped you reduce your interest. You won because you were paying less, and he won because he got to collect the interest that might have gone to other sources.

"The second way it shows teamwork is that you can now be part of Pete and Jenny's team to help them reduce their debt. You've just given them an idea on how to meet their goal of having no VISA balance in six months. They should visit their banker and look at ways of reducing their interest.

"Any other ideas on who you could get on your team, Pete and Jenny?" Steve asked the couple.

Pete's face lit up. "Jenny's father is excellent at saving money. He's always giving me advice on where to find bargains."

Jenny was shocked. Pete hadn't said anything good about her father in years. Jenny could only respond with "It's about time you started taking some of his advice!"

Chris spoke up, "So, Steve. Now we've got a scorecard, a game plan and a team assembled. It looks like we're sure to score those goals!"

Steve replied, "We're almost there, Chris, but there are two more steps. First, we've got to get past the wet tennis balls and then we've got to put the puck in the net."

"Huh?" Jenny offered, confused.

Steve went on, "The fourth step of the goal-scoring process is to identify the obstacles and determine the best path around them. In street hockey, one of the obstacles we frequently encounter is wet tennis balls. Your buddy might get a face full of water if he tries to stop one, or the garage door will get covered with round tennis-ball marks if you're playing in the driveway and you keep missing the net. So, at this point, I like to write down the wet tennis balls (or you can just call them obstacles, Jenny) representing the problems that we could very well face."

Jenny pondered. "I understand how wet tennis balls can make a game less fun, but what would be a wet tennis ball in our example?"

Pete spoke up. "I can think of one right away. In fact, it's been bugging me for a while, and I don't know how to get around it. The first "wet tennis ball" in our goal would be, How can we avoid adding new purchases on the VISA card? The balance didn't get up to $900 by itself. Every time I've tried to pay it down in the past, it hasn't worked because in the meantime I've added to the VISA card balance. How can I get past this?"

Steve asked the rest of them, "Any ideas, team?"

Chris said, "Why not just cut up the card?"

Steve loved that answer. "Fantastic! As you're going along, you'll meet other wet tennis balls. The important thing is to get around them, or over them, or through them. And use your team as much as you can!"

Mark wondered aloud, "What's the final step, Steve?"

Steve said, "You've got to drop the puck and start moving. Then keep moving forward until you've scored your goal. Pete and Jenny mentioned they want to get rid of their credit card debt so they can sleep at night. Many others need to get rid of debt so they can move closer to their retirement goals. Whatever your goals are, or whatever they become, it's important to start moving towards accomplishing them today. If your plan is six months, and the balance is not yet zero in six months, keep going towards the goal."

Jenny smiled. "You really know how to put the fun in funancial planning, Steve."

Steve pulled out some more sheets with hockey rinks in the background. These outlined a review of the week's lesson. Each of the students took one to help them remember the goal-scoring process.

Scoring Your Goals

Make a scorecard
- Write down your goals.
- Add the reason you want to score this goal.
- Review them regularly.

Make a game plan to score each goal
- Break the goal into baby steps.
- Put steps in logical order to move the puck up the ice.

Get a good team behind you
- Ask others for help.
- Look for win-win relationships.

Identify the Wet tennis balls
- Lay out the obstacles.
- Determine methods around, over or through obstacles.

Put the puck in the net
- Take action to move towards scoring the goal.

Practice Session 3
Play the Full Sixty Minutes

The next Tuesday came quickly. Pete and Jenny had planned on discussing how to prioritize their goals, but hadn't had the time yet to do it. As everyone sat down, Chris threw out,

"Did anyone catch the game last night between the Canucks and the Sharks? It was 1-1 after the first period, and then 2-2 after the second. It looked like it was going to go down to the wire. But in the third period, San Jose fell apart. Vancouver ended up winning 7-2. What a blowout!"

"You know what they say," Pete said. "You've got to play the full sixty minutes if you want to win."

Steve began, "Let's get started. Did everyone write some game plans for their highest priority goals?"

Pete replied, "We haven't had time yet, Steve, but we're going to do it this week."

Steve continued, "It's okay to delay things a little, but I'm going to show you tonight that the earlier you get started on your financial goals, the better. Chris, you're in an ideal position to start saving. You're 18 and you have your whole life ahead of you. If you were to start investing a dollar a day on investments that return 10 percent per year, how long do you think it would be before you're a millionaire?"

Chris guessed, "It would probably be. . .100 years?"

Steve replied, "It's good that you're guessing a nice round number, and that's correct if your investments are only returning 5 percent. At 10 percent, though, you would actually have a million dollars by the time you're 74."

Mark chipped in, "That's all well and good, but getting 10 percent on your investments isn't guaranteed. Most of the banks are suggesting 6-8 percent as a reasonable rate of return when planning your future."

"Thanks for pointing that out," Steve responded. "The banks like to show conservative rates of interest. Another example that the banks like to show is two people who decide at different points in their life to start saving money. Let's use Chris, and we'll pretend he has a twin brother John. If Chris starts putting $2,000 a year into investments returning 8 percent (we'll use the bank's figures) at age 21, and then stops at age thirty—" (he bent over his laptop) "—he'll have over $145,000 by the time he's fifty. If John, his twin brother, waits to start investing his $2,000 a year until he's thirty-one, and then continues until he's fifty, he'll have just under $99,000."

Mark said, "Wait a minute. John has put in $40,000 and Chris has only put in $20,000. Don't you mean John has $46,000 more?"

Steve replied, "No, Mark. This is the magic of compound interest! By getting the money in earlier, you don't need to put as much in to get more out. Time allows the interest to accumulate. Compounding means that not only is the $20,000 making interest, but the interest is making interest as well.

"The first advantage of getting started early, then, is that your money will work for you through compound interest. That's the magic which allows a dollar a day to grow into a million dollars within your lifetime."

Chris looked puzzled. "Anybody can save a dollar a day. Why aren't all retirees millionaires?"

Steve responded, "That's an excellent question! Why don't we ask your father? Mark, why aren't you going to be a millionaire when you retire?"

Mark grumbled, "When I was young, the last thing I thought about was retiring. Any money I made went towards getting married, then supporting my family and then preparing for your college education. I'm doing well now, though, and I'm learning more about investing, so I can increase my rates of return."

"And I think that's typical of a lot of North Americans," Steve remarked. "It's hard to plan for the future when you're trying to struggle through the day-to-day expenses. This brings us to the next advantage of getting started early, which is that your habit of saving for the future gets ingrained at an earlier age. We are all creatures of habit. If we are in the habit of living day to day, and trying to get by each month, then we'll tend to stay in that habit until something stronger pulls us out of it. If you can get started early with the habit of saving and investing your money, then that habit will pay off huge dividends in the future.

"The third major advantage of getting started early is that your knowledge of investments will have time to grow and mature. We've already spoken about different rates of return. To get higher rates of return often involves changing your investment strategy, and thereby taking more risk. The earlier you're involved with investing, the longer your timeframe for learning how to get higher rates of return."

Pete broke in, "I think you've done a good job of convincing Chris to start early. You've spoken about compound interest, developing good financial habits, and having a more mature knowledge of investments and investment vehicles. But what about me? I'm almost forty and can't afford 56 years to save a dollar a day! What can I do to improve my finances?"

Steve responded, " This brings me into the next part of this lesson, which is more about good financial habits that anyone making money and planning for their retirement should follow.

"Does anyone here brush their teeth every day?" Steve asked the group. They all nodded suspiciously. Steve looked at Mark and said, "Why do you follow this time-consuming habit?"

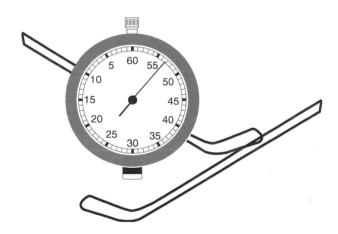

Mark replied, "Because I want my teeth to outlast me. If I take care of them every day, my dentist tells me they should last a very long time."

"Excellent response!" Steve said enthusiastically. "Who else wants their teeth to outlast them?" Everyone's hand went up, and there was a bit of shuffling and rustling in the room. It wasn't immediately obvious where this was going. "And who wants their money to outlast them?" Steve continued.

The group looked a bit surprised. Jenny and Mark were quick to raise their hands, and then Pete joined them. Chris finally caught on, and raised his hand as well, and then added, "Tell us what we have to do, Coach."

"Since you only spend a few minutes each day brushing your teeth, I won't expect you to spend much more time on your finances. One of the first habits you'll have to develop is tracking your money—where it comes from and where it goes. Every time you make a purchase, or make money, categorize it."

"Is this leading to a budget?" Pete asked.

"Yes, it is," Steve replied. "A budget, though, depends on your knowing where you're going to spend the money, and then comparing your actual expenses with the predicted expenses. Before we get to that, we need to concentrate on monitoring our expenses.

"First, when you earn or spend money, write it down. Most people don't have more than five or six purchases a day. Every time you purchase something, verify the price. With computers nowadays, you never know if the sale price is going to be taken into account or not. Then write it down in a little black book, or get a copy of the receipt for later filing, or do both.

"Make sure you note how the purchase was made. Was it cash, debit, or credit card? You should also categorize it while you've got a chance. Was it a business expense? Did you spend the money on a household expense? Here's an example of my categories, and how I log expenses." Steve showed the group a copy of his daily records.

Date	Expense	Amount	Category	Type	Priority
Jan. 5/03	Coffee & donuts	$6.43	Misc.	Cash	3
Jan. 5/03	Car repair	$323.22	Car	VISA	1
Jan. 6/03	Savings	$250	Self	WD	1
Jan. 6/03	Mortgage payment	$675	Home	WD	1
Jan. 6/03	Clothes – children	$43.56	Home	Debit	2
Jan. 7/03	Groceries	$143.25	Food	Debit	1
Jan. 7/03	Movie & snacks	$32.20	Entertainment	Debit	2
Jan. 7/03	Food bank donation	$50	Charity	Cash	1

Daily Expense Form

"The number of categories I've got is nine (in honor of Gordie Howe), and the reasons for some of these categories will become clearer as we move forward. There is no one correct method of categorizing expenses. You've all got to find what works for you. It's important, though, that you start recording where your money is going! You'd be surprised how a daily coffee or two adds up over the month." Steve handed out some little black books with gold lettering on them.

"What does $HM stand for?" Chris asked naively.

"Street Hockey Millionaires!" Mark and Pete responded enthusiastically.

"That's right." Steve grinned. "I want you all to be part of my team. To become a street hockey millionaire, you're going to have to track where your money is going, and here's the perfect vehicle to do it. Now, let's talk about the B-word."

Pete whined, "Not the budget."

Steve replied, "Yes, it's time to look at the budget. If it will help, you can think of them as early season predictions, just like in hockey. Many of your expenses, especially the larger ones like your mortgage and loan payments, are very predictable. You'd be surprised how few of your monthly expenses will actually vary."

"Yeah, Steve," Pete agreed. "But it just takes one surprise to ruin your predictions."

"There's no way to avoid surprises," Steve resumed. "We'll be looking at defensive maneuvers next week to reduce their impact on big-ticket expenses like house and car repairs. First, let's look at budgeting.

"A budget is a method of ensuring you have money to pay for the important things in your life. Your financial plans and goals can have a very long time horizon (like Chris's 47 years to retirement and Pete's 8 years to save for his son's education). A budget is done in a much shorter timeframe to ensure the money will be there in the long term. It involves calculating the income (or predicting it, for self-employed professionals like Mark), and then determining which category the money will be partitioned to. That's the first half of budgeting – making the predictions.

"The second half should be easy if you're using your $HM black books. The second step is to write down the actual amount you've spent beside your prediction. Let me show you an example.

		Jan		Feb		Mar	
Net Income		2500		2500		2500	
Expense Categories	Budget	Actual	Budget	Actual	Budget	Actual	Budget
Savings	250	250	250				
Charity	50	50	50				
Business	100	76	100				
Car	100	363	100				
Mortgage	675	675	675				
Groceries	300	286	300				
Home	825	817	825				
Entertainment	50	32	50				
Misc.	150	169	150				
Actual Expense		2718					
Savings/Loss		-218					
Retirement Goals	Age 65	Save $1.2M			Each month: $225		

Monthly Budget Form

"At the end of each month," Steve explained, "fill in the actual expenses for the previous month, and the expected expenses for the next month. So, on January 31st, for example, write down the actual expenses for January, and the expected expenses for February."

Pete spoke up, "Does anyone ever have the expected equal the actual?"

Steve smiled. "Everybody gets better the more they do it. Just like in hockey, success in budgeting takes discipline."

"There are no excuses in hockey!" Jenny joked, imitating Pete. The gang laughed at her surprisingly accurate impression.

"The problem I've got, Steve," Pete noted, "is that I get paid every two weeks. My month gets broken up into these weird chunks of time that don't make a whole lot of sense."

Steve nodded, "Again it comes down to customization. It would probably be easier for you to plan on a two-week or four-week schedule. Don't give up though, Pete, just because it seems hard. Find something that works. Your future is too important to neglect just because your income and your expenses don't necessarily jive."

"Now, I've mentioned two good habits to incorporate into your lives – namely, tracking your daily expenses and budgeting monthly. There are two more good habits that lead from the first two expense categories on my daily expense form – pay yourself first and give money to your favorite charity.

"Paying yourself first is a fairly lengthy topic, so let's leave that to the end. Our third habit worth developing is to give money to your favorite charity. Does everyone give money to charity now?"

Chris shook his head, "I've got no money to give."

Pete looked at Jenny and said, "Jenny keeps telling me to be more generous. To cut expenses, though, I need to cut back on charitable donations or else we'll have no money for the essentials."

Steve replied, "You'd be surprised at how non-essential some of your essentials are. The thing about money is that it has to flow. The more you give, the more you receive. Does anyone here consider themselves wealthy?"

No one lifted a hand.

"Wealth is a relative term," Steve went on. "Millions of people in this world earn less than a thousand dollars a year. In North America, thousands of people are homeless, and thousands more live in government-subsidized housing because they can't afford rent. Everyone in this room, except maybe Chris, should consider themselves very wealthy already.

We live in an area of the world which is filled with abundance."

Steve was distracted when Jenny stood up and started moving her hips. Pete asked her what she was doing.

"A 'bun dance,'" Jenny answered.

"A what?"

"I was just thinking of how lucky we really are," Jenny said, "and to celebrate our abundance, I'm doing a 'bun dance.'" The rest of the group seemed to think it would be fun to join in. With the exception of Chris, though, the men just didn't have the rhythm for it.

As the dance break ended, Steve started again. "We were speaking about giving to charity. The first benefit is the feeling inside when you're known as a giver. Give to everyone who asks. If you don't have as much money as they're asking for, give them what you feel you can afford. If you're convinced you have no money to give, give them your time.

"The second reason for giving to charity is that money is like water. It needs to move. If you give money to people less fortunate, then they'll spend it on their essentials, and the money will continue to flow. If you lock away every dime you've got, then the money becomes stagnant and stops flowing.

"Next, let's discuss paying yourself first. When your paycheck arrives, who do you pay first?"

Jenny responded with, "Our mortgage payments are synchronized to be deducted the same day as Pete's paycheck gets deposited. We don't even see the money. That way, we don't get a chance to spend it before it's needed."

Steve looked meaningfully at Pete and Jenny. "What if you put money in your savings right away? Before you got a chance to spend it?"

Jenny replied, "Well, we wouldn't even see it. So it would be safe from spending."

Pete responded, "Steve, you don't understand. We're having a hard time making ends meet now. How much money do you want us to put away?"

Steve said calmly, "As a general rule, putting away 10 percent of your income is a great vehicle to ensure your money outlasts you. If you save 10 percent of your income, do you realize how much you'll have over time? We've already discussed how compound interest can help your savings grow. Imagine if your savings are bigger and growing.

"North Americans are not prone to doing this. Instead, they want a new car, a new house, a new DVD player, etc, etc. They don't think long-term until it's too late. That's why over 90 percent of us won't have the money we need to retire comfortably.

"Coincidentally, this brings us to our last topic of the evening. To properly prepare for the last period of our lives – that is, our retirement –we need to know how much we're going to need, and how we're going to get there."

Jenny interrupted, "I was speaking to my Dad about this last week. When he retired, he had a great pension. He never had to save very much money because he knew he had that safety net."

"Well, Jenny," Steve responded, "many new companies have different pension strategies than the older companies. Nowadays, people have a much longer life expectancy than they did twenty or thirty years ago. So the retirement period is going to last longer. Companies are not as eager to give life-long pensions, so they are moving to other forms of pensions. The first thing you should do is to examine what pension options your company has. Take advantage of what

your company is offering, and factor that into your cal-
culation of your retirement needs. Speak with the
Benefits personnel if you have questions. Two things
you'll want to check are the percentage of your final
salary that the pension will cover, and whether the
pension is indexed with inflation. Often, pensions will
cover 65 to 85 percent of your salary. Many seniors
want to travel when they retire, and hope to be in a
position to do so. You might want to consider topping
up those pension plans.

"For self-employed individuals, like Mark, and for
employees of newer companies, like Pete, the pension
plans are non-existent, or dependent on employee contributions. Governments have realized that many of
their citizens will retire broke if they don't follow a reg-
imented retirement savings plan. So they've instituted
tax-deduction and tax-deferral programs to encourage
citizens to save money for retirement. In Canada, the
plan is called Registered Retirement Savings Plan
(RRSP), and in the U.S., the main plan is called an
Individual Retirement Account (IRA). For both the
RRSP and the IRA, individuals can make annual contributions up to certain limits. Contributions may be
eligible for tax deductions, and all gains made within
the plan are tax-deferred until the individual retires.
There is, however, a penalty with the IRA if it is withdrawn before the individual turns 59½ years.

"Having taxes on the gains deferred in these plans
adds tremendously to the value. I mentioned earlier the
effect of compound interest. Since the gains are not
taxed, the interest is all staying in the account, so that
interest will continue to compound and grow. The tax
is applied when the money is withdrawn. Pete and
Jenny, you should consider both having equal retirement accounts. That way, when the money is

withdrawn, the income tax is split between the two of you, rather than Pete paying more tax on his income. In Canada, this can be done through a Spousal RRSP. Chris, whether you start working in the U.S. or Canada, make sure you're familiar with the penalties and benefits before you start contributing to an IRA or an RRSP. Whichever way you go, start right away!

"Let's look at calculating how much we need to retire comfortably, and then we need to calculate the minimum amount we should be putting away each month to meet that goal.

"When I first did this, there were a lot of manual calculations. Nowadays, you can go to the Internet and get the information in minutes. One of my favorite spots to go is the retirement calculator on my bank's web site. It works great for Canadians, and I'm sure that banks and investment firms in other countries have similar calculators on their web sites. This calculator tells us that if Pete and Jenny want to retire with $60,000 annually in the future, then they will need over $1.3 million dollars in their retirement fund to achieve their goal. This is assuming that the inflation rate stays at 3 percent, and that the government pension plan will contribute 30 percent of their retirement savings."

Pete injected, "What if I don't trust the government? Let's take their contributions out of the picture to be safe." The number Pete and Jenny needed to save shot up to over 1.9 million dollars.

"Let's look at Chris's numbers," Steve said. "With no government pension, Chris will need 3.5 million dollars to retire at age 65, using all the same assumptions as Pete had. With a government pension plan contributing 30 percent of Chris' retirement income, the number comes down to 2.2 million."

Mark joked, "You're going to have to start the Street Hockey Multi-Millionaires' Club, Chris. What about me, Steve? I want to retire at sixty with an income of $50,000."

Steve did some calculations. "It looks as if you'll need $846,000 with government contributions, or $994,000 without government contributions. Now, you'll notice from the budget forms I showed you earlier that your retirement goal should be listed there. These numbers should give you more of an incentive to save at least 10 percent.

"Speaking of which, the last thing I need to cover tonight is the amount of money you're going to need to put away each month to meet those lofty retirement goals. Even though I said 10 percent before, we're about to find out just what chunk of your income it will take to maintain your current lifestyles. The calculations we use for retirement can also be applied to goals for financing your children's education, Pete.

"One of the things I have to mention here is that there are a few numbers that will remain constant, and there are a few numbers that will vary. The constants are your target retirement age and your target retirement salary. The variables are inflation and the rate of return on your investments. A generally accepted value for the inflation rate is 3 percent. But this could change, and could affect your target retirement goals significantly. Likewise, if you can get a better rate of return than the 6 to 8 percent which the banks predict, then you can significantly increase your retirement savings. We're looking at timeframes here from 10 to 25 to 47 years. Don't go thinking you can set a goal to put away money tonight and stay with that for the rest of your lives. You're going to have to review it frequently, at least annually, and take note of inflation rates and your rates of return.

"When we start talking about offense in a few weeks, I'll get into methods to increase your rates of return. For now, let's assume the inflation rate will stay at 3 percent, and that your rate of return will average 8 percent for the remainder of your non-retirement years. Mark, let's look at you first. You've done a good job of putting away $300,000, and your retirement goal in ten years is to have a portfolio of $994,000, right?"

Mark nodded, "Yeah, Steve, I'd rather have the extra money in case the government messes up or changes its rules."

"Using some tables my Uncle Ken passed down to me," Steve said, "Mark, you'll need to save $2,000 per month. Since your mortgage is paid off, and your kids are heading off to college, it hopefully won't be too difficult.

"Chris, you'll want to put away at least 10 percent of your income until you have a better appreciation of what you'll want in your retirement.

"Pete and Jenny, you'll need $1,500 per month. That's assuming you can get an 8 percent return on your investments."

Pete responded, "Ouch! What if I just spend 15 years in retirement?"

Steve replied, "Isn't it better to have enough money until you turn ninety, and then die at eighty, than it is to have enough money until you turn eighty, and then die at ninety?"

Pete smiled, "Fair enough! What if you move away, and there's no one to help us with these calculations?"

Steve said, "There are a lot of resources on the Internet to help you calculate your retirement needs. As well, there are financial planners and investment professionals who can help you determine your needs. Just remember to shop around for someone you trust, and get more than one opinion to make sure it's reliable. On the Internet, I found one web site telling me you need $24,000 per year, while another web site is telling me you need just $7,000 per year."

Jenny considered the lesson for the evening and said, "Steve, you've told us to start early, keep our heads up by developing good habits, and prepare for the end game. In hockey, don't they call that 'Playing the full sixty minutes'?" Again her impersonation of Pete was dead on.

As usual, Jenny had gotten in the last word before Steve distributed his review sheets with the hockey rink in the background. The group disassembled with an even greater wealth of knowledge.

Play the Full Sixty Minutes

Start early
 Take advantage of compound interest.

Start with the proper habits.

Gain more knowledge.

Develop good habits

Monitor spending daily.

Budget monthly or near-monthly to ensure long-term goals will be met.

Give to charity.

Pay yourself first.

Prepare for the end game

Know the amount you need to retire.

Calculate a monthly payment plan to get there.

Practice Session 4
Set up a Good Defense

Steve looked at the gang of financial students. He hadn't been sure how they would take the news about their large portfolio goals and their target savings goals. They had had a week to soak in the information, but he thought he'd begin by testing the water. "Has everyone had some time to think about their retirement goals?"

"They certainly are large, Steve," Jenny replied. "But we're much happier to find out now than ten years from now. Imagine if we'd gone ten more years without realizing that we need almost two million dollars to retire comfortably."

Mark added, "I thought I was ahead of the game in regards to my retirement. I'm going to have to do a lot more if I want to stay on track for retiring at sixty. What are we going to talk about tonight?"

Steve was relieved. His students had taken the new knowledge gracefully, and seemed even more eager to learn how to improve their financial situation. Steve answered Mark's question. "Your savings are basically the difference between what you spend and what you earn. To increase your savings, you need to either spend less or earn more. Ideally, you should be doing both. Earning more money is what I like to refer to as 'going on the offense.' Spending less is achieved by 'setting up the defense.'"

Pete jumped in. "That makes sense. When I play hockey, I'm an offensive player. When you talked about increasing my savings, the first thing I thought of was how I could make more money. I'm excited, Steve! Let's discuss offense."

But Steve rebuffed Pete's comments. "Offense is important, and it's one of the ways to increase your savings. For most people, it is hard to give up things they currently enjoy. It seems much easier to just make more money. However, if they don't change the way they think and act, an increase in salary won't necessarily increase the savings; their spending habits will similarly increase with their income. Let's look at what I mean. Pete, how much money have you and Jenny earned in the last 15 years?"

Pete thought about it, and then did some calculations. He responded, "Including salary, stock options and money made in selling our house, I would say that we've made . . . can this be right? It looks like we've made over 1.1 million dollars. Wow! Where did it all go?"

Mark was doing similar calculations. With ten more years of experience, his earnings were over 1.5 million dollars.

"It looks like you've already made a lot of money," Steve commented. "When you retire, though, it's not the money you've made that matters, it's the money you've kept. A number of things should be done to set up your defense to ensure that your savings will grow."

"What do we need to defend ourselves against?" Mark put in.

Steve replied, "In order to help your savings grow, you need to defend yourselves against overspending, high-interest debt, unfair taxes, inflation, unexpected events and investment losses. Let's go through these subjects one at a time.

"The first point is defense against overspending. If you develop the habits we talked about last week (like budgeting and paying yourself first), you're well on your way to beating the overspending bug. There are many other things you can do as well. You need to shop around, and get the best deal you can on purchases. Speaking of purchases, the first things I'd like you to examine are your largest expenses, like a house and a car.

"When buying a car, there are several things to consider. Paying cash will definitely save you money. If you buy a $20,000 car with a 7.9 percent interest-rate loan over five years, your monthly payment will be $404.57. You'll actually be paying $24,274.20 for that $20,000 car."

"What about those 0.9 percent deals?" Pete asked.

Steve responded, "Buying a car with a loan that has a low interest rate is better than buying a car with a loan that has a high interest rate. Realize this, though: the car salesman will be glad to lower the price if you're paying in cash. They're probably losing money by offering the low interest rate loans, so your cash offer should get you a better price.

"Shop around when you're looking for cars, and never buy the car on the same day you first test-drive it. Let the price and the features sink in before making the decision to buy. Consider buying used cars versus the flashy new cars. Cars tend to depreciate quickly. With many cars nowadays lasting over 10 years, a used car which is two years old and 25 to 30 percent cheaper than its new car equivalent can be a good bargain.

"Buying a house with cash is rare these days, so let's assume you're going to get a mortgage. Again, you want to reduce the interest you're going to have to pay, and there are many ways to do this. The first thing you should do is shop around for the best mortgage rates. Often, banks will post rates for high-risk homeowners. If you've got a steady job and a good credit record, simply ask for, and expect, a lower rate than the posted rates (and don't forget to mention your steady income and good credit record). Go to at least three different banks to get a sense of what a fair rate is, and to determine how well you'll get along with your banker. You can also look in your local paper for companies offering low-rate mortgages. If you want the low rates, but would rather deal with your local bank, get the low-rate company to fax or give you a hard copy of a quote with the low rate they're offering. Then approach your bank, and tell them you'd like the low rate but would like to stick with them. Ask them if they can meet that rate.

"A second step to reduce the interest you'll pay is to apply a larger down payment. This will reduce the interest you'll have to pay in future years. In countries like Canada, you can even be charged a penalty if you put down less than 25 percent of the price of the house. This penalty (called CMHC insurance) can really add up when added to the mortgage principal.

"A third method for reducing the interest you'll pay on your mortgage is to reduce the length of time you take to pay it off. If you are looking at getting a $100,000 mortgage at an interest rate of 7 percent, reducing the length from 25 years to 15 years will actually save you $49,257 over the life of the mortgage!

"Another great method to reduce your mortgage is to get the best price you can when purchasing the house. Shop around. I've had friends who have looked at over 75 houses just to find the right combination of features and price.

"The last piece of advice I can give you to help you defend yourself against spending too much on your mortgage is to look at paying more frequently. Pete, you mentioned you're paid bi-weekly. If you arrange with your bank to pay half the monthly rate every two weeks, you'll reduce the amount of time it will take to pay the mortgage, and the amount of interest you'll pay on the mortgage. Let's look at an example of a 25-year mortgage with a fixed interest rate of 7 percent. If you change from paying monthly to paying half the monthly payment every two weeks, your mortgage will be paid off in twenty years and six months, and you'll save $23,999 in interest charges. Plus, it will be easier for you to budget if your mortgage payments are taken out at the same time your paycheck is deposited.

"That should cover the purchase of your car and house. Next, I'm going to speak to you about taking care of your house and car. Doing preventive maintenance on the house and car can save hundreds of dollars, maybe even thousands, down the road. As well, it's a great way to avoid unexpected expenses. You can save even more money if you do the maintenance yourself. If your heating and cooling bills seem high, make sure the house is well defended against the outdoor temperature. Seal the windows and doors well, since they're the easiest way for the indoor air to escape and for the outdoor air to get in."

"I know what you mean, Steve," Mark chimed in. "Three years ago, I fixed the weather-stripping on my doors, and had new windows installed. My energy bills went down almost 20 percent!"

"While saving money on your house and car can be financially rewarding," Steve went on, "there are other things to protect yourself against overspending. Chris mentioned a great defensive maneuver a few weeks ago. Do you remember what that was, Chris?"

Chris looked dumbfounded. The information had been coming at him so fast and furious, he wasn't sure he knew what Steve was thinking. Suddenly, the light bulb came on and Chris declared, "Cut up your credit cards!"

"Exactly!" Steve said. "In business, debt is used to produce products or prepare services so the money can be recovered later. With credit cards, personal debt has become a bad habit. Consumers now use credit cards to purchase things they really can't afford. I spoke before about buying a car in cash and about the money you'd end up spending on interest if you took out a five-year loan at 7.9 percent. The same logic applies to furniture, appliances and other big-ticket items. Keep in mind that a furniture set costing $2,000, purchased on a standard VISA or MasterCard with an interest rate of 18.5 percent, now costs $2,621.16 when paid over three years. We spoke before about a 15 percent return on our investments being good. Banks are getting a return of 18.5 percent from consumers through credit card spending. Department stores are getting 28 percent in many cases.

"This leads nicely to the next element of a good defense: defending yourself against high interest rates. Many young people these days are all too familiar with debt by the time they finish college or university. The costs of tuition and residence continue to climb, and more and more people are borrowing to get a good education. As they enter the workforce, many young people continue to borrow. They borrow large amounts for their weddings, their first home, and the appliances and furniture to fill their new home. Hopefully, I've shown you that all this debt is keeping you from reaching your savings goal. The interest you're paying on this debt continues to grow until the debts are paid off.

"While it's become socially accepted (maybe even encouraged) to borrow money for big-ticket items through credit cards and loans, it's not wise financially. In an ideal world, people would pay for all personal items in cash, and avoid the debt trap. Since we don't live in a cash-only society, let's examine debt, and see how we can defend against the biggest culprit, high interest.

"The first thing you should do is keep records of all your loans. Get a ledger, or some other book that has lines and rules, to store all the information in one place. Write down all credit card debt, mortgages and loan information. Include interest rates, terms of payment and any pertinent dates related to the debt. An example of a pertinent date is the date when interest rates are set to change. Many credit cards are now offering reduced rates to entice new cardholders. These reduced rates vary between 0 and 6 percent, but the reduced rates are often good for only six months. After that, the rates skyrocket to the standard 17.5 or 18.5 percent."

"That's quite a jump!" Jenny exclaimed.

"It sure is," Steve responded, "so you have to watch out for those dates. Here's a sneak at what Pete and Jenny's debt record looks like:"

Lender	Interest Rate	Limit	Owing	Special Dates
Credit Card #1	5.9%	$5,000	$150	May 1/03 – rate increase
Credit Card #2	18.5%	$3,000	$900	
Department Store Card	28.5 %	$2,000	$235	
Car Loan	7.9%	$20,000 principal	$404 monthly payment	Oct. 15/04 – maturity date
Mortgage	7 %	$140,000 principal	$989.49 monthly	March 1/06 – renewal date

Debt Record for Pete and Jenny Smith

"Keeping records may give you better control of your debt, but you also have to act towards reducing the debt so your savings can grow. Which of the debts on this debt record should be your highest priority?"

Mark spoke up, "If we want to defend ourselves against high interest, then the loans with the highest interest should be our biggest priority."

Steve nodded, "Definitely! In our example, there are department store credit cards charging 28.5 percent, while another credit card is only charging 5.9 percent. A good maneuver to save money instantly is to transfer the balance from the department store card to the low-interest credit card."

"While we're discussing credit cards," Steve continued, "I want to mention that several banks offer a credit card with a lower interest rate (often between 9 and 12 percent). The catch here is that the annual fee is usually higher than the card with the higher interest rate. If you're looking at carrying debt on your credit card, you'd probably be better off paying the higher annual fee to save the money on interest."

Chris put forward, "Maybe I should never get a credit card then."

Steve responded, "Having a credit card is good for emergency situations. Just stick to one, pay it off every month and remember to use it responsibly."

Mark got in a little dig. "That's not the only thing you need to use responsibly."

Chris looked at him and whined, "Oh, Dad."

As Pete and Jenny giggled, Steve went on, "Banks offer many vehicles to help their customers reduce interest. A consolidation loan, which we discussed before, is a great example. The bank agrees to pay off your credit cards, and then lends you the money at a reduced rate, often for a two- or three-year term. This helps you defend yourself against high interest, and the bank is now collecting all the interest on your loan. You do have to apply for this type of loan. If you get rejected, find out why. I've been rejected at one branch of a bank, and then been accepted for the same loan at a cross-town branch of the same bank. Banks make very good money through their loan programs. Speak with a loan officer or the manager at your bank to determine other methods to reduce interest. With so many people borrowing, banks are competitive and often come up with new products and services. Having a good relationship with people at the bank can help you stay on top of the latest offerings, as well as increasing your chances of success at reducing your interest rate.

"While debt is something we can hope to avoid, taxes are something we can't avoid. A large percentage of the money we make will go towards taxes. Everyone needs to pay their fair share, and the tax laws are written to allow this. There are, however, some ways to prevent spending more than your fair share on taxes. The first thing you should do is keep good records. Whatever you're allowed tax deductions for, whether it be charity or political contributions or investment losses, make sure you keep the paperwork required to make the right deduction. The same goes for your income. Keep good records so you know you're paying the fair share.

"Tax deferral programs, like the IRA in the U.S. and the RRSP in Canada, are great for delaying taxes. The equity in these plans also grow on a tax-deferred basis, so the principal invested is larger. Look into growing as much of your retirement money in these plans as possible.

"Governments often give small businesses tax breaks. If you're setting up your own company, make sure you take advantage of the tax breaks that you're entitled to. Again, good records of your revenues and your expenditures are crucial to ensure you're paying no more than your fair share of taxes.

"In the United States, there are municipal bonds which are non-taxable. If you invest in these bonds, your real rate of return is much greater than similar bonds that are taxable. For instance, if you have a municipal bond giving you a rate of return of 5 percent, and your tax rate is 30 percent, then it would be equivalent to a taxable investment which is giving you a return of 7.14 percent.

"Taxes are already a big drain on your savings. Don't allow them to become a bigger drain than they need to be.

"The next opponent we need to defend ourselves against is inflation. If you hide your money in your mattress for 10 years, you won't lose any money, but the value of the money will actually decrease. Your spending power will be less because the prices of goods and services have gone up. To beat inflation, your savings have to increase by at least the same rate as inflation just to maintain your spending rate. Let's look at a few expenses for this year, and see how they'll compare ten, twenty and thirty years from now. With an inflation rate of 3 percent, you can expect these prices in the years to come." Everyone leaned closer to look at the tables Steve pointed to.

Expense	Current Cost	Cost in Ten Years	Cost in Twenty Years	Cost in Thirty Years
Movie and Snack	$20.00	$26.88	$36.12	$48.55
Washer/Dryer	$1000.00	$1,343.92	$1,806.11	$2,427.26
New Car	$20,000.00	$26,878,33	$36,122.22	$48,545.25

Effect of 3 Percent Inflation

"If however, the inflation rate increases to 5 percent, you can expect the following rise in prices:

Expense	Current Cost	Cost in Ten Years	Cost in Twenty Years	Cost in Thirty Years
Movie and Snack	$20.00	$32.58	$53.07	$86.44
Washer/Dryer	$1,000.00	$1,628.89	$2,653.30	$4,321.94
New Car	$20,000.00	$32,577.89	$53,065.95	$86,438.85

Effect of 5 Percent Inflation

"As you can see, if the inflation rate takes a modest jump from 3 to 5 percent, it can have quite an effect on your future spending. It's important to get your money working for you as quickly as possible, because inflation is not waiting around. Quick question: If the inflation rate is 3 percent, what rate of return do you need to get on your investments to beat inflation?"

Pete was the first to respond, "Our rate of return has to be greater than 3 percent!" Chris nodded his head.

Steve grinned, "Unfortunately, we get taxed on our investment income. Depending on your tax rate, and the tax laws of the day, you'd probably have to make at least 4 percent. If we use the example of a 30 percent tax bracket, you would have to make at least 4.2 percent on your investments just to account for inflation."

Pete broke in, "But Steve, if I put my money in a Registered Retirement Savings Plan, I don't have to worry about taxes."

"Sorry, Pete," Steve said apologetically, "but that plan doesn't keep you from paying taxes. It only helps you defer taxes until you withdraw the money. When you take the money out of your plan, you'll have to pay the taxes then. So, you see, you still need to defend yourself against inflation. The tax laws may change, so you have to keep on top of them.

"A good example of a tax law changing in Canada is the capital gains tax. When I started out, money made on capital gains (like gains from stocks, bonds and real estate investments) had a lifetime limit of $100,000 tax-free. Now, the law in Canada states that 50 percent of your capital gains are tax-exempt. If you move to another country, you'll have to check their tax laws and their inflation rates to know how to defend your money against inflation there."

"All this talk about defense reminds me," Chris remarked. "The Red Wings are playing the Rockies tonight. Can we take a TV timeout to let the knowledge about overspending and inflation sink in?"

Pete didn't wait for Steve's answer. He flipped on the converter to the game. "The score's tied at four, and we're still in the second period. Learn some defense, boys!" The group laughed at his remarks. While Pete had earlier spoken about the glories of offense, he was now screaming at the players to be more defensive.

Steve grinned, recognizing that he'd made at least a small impact on Pete. Time would be a better judge, Steve knew, as Pete would have to remember to be defensive for the full sixty minutes. The second period ended 5-5. Pete turned off the television and the gang returned their attention to Steve.

"Defending yourself against overspending, high interest debt, unfair taxes and inflation are the first four moves. The fifth opponent you need to defend your savings against is any unexpected event. While no one expects to die before they retire, many people do. The last thing you'll want to do is leave your family with an empty net."

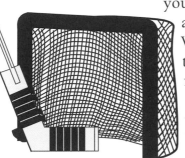

"An empty net?" Jenny questioned.

"What I mean by that, Jenny, is that you need two things to protect your family when you die: a will and some life insurance. Without a will, the state could decide how your estate, including your assets and your children, would be divided up. Without life insurance, your spouse could be left with huge bills and a loss of steady income. Let's look first at a will, and then we'll cover life insurance.

"A will is a legal document that outlines how you wish your estate to be divided when you die. It needs to outline what actions you'd like others to take at your death. If you die without a valid will in place, you die intestate."

"Intestate!" injected Mark, "That sounds nasty!"

"What intestate means," Steve went on, "is that the government uses the laws of the day to decide how to settle your estate. To defend your loved ones against unexpected settlements, a will is necessary. It's really not that complicated either. It's just a plan for how you want your assets to be divided, and who will get how much.

"Before writing the will, take some time to think about where you'd want your money to go. Do you want it all to go to your wife? Your children? Your poor niece? Your favorite charity?"

"I'd like to leave my money to the Toronto Maple Leafs," Pete smirked, "so they could buy a good goalie for a change!"

"I wouldn't make fun of the Leafs, Pete," Mark returned. "They've knocked your beloved Senators out of the playoffs a few times now."

"Speaking of wills," Jenny said, "I see ads on television showing a home kit. Is that the best way to go about it? To do it yourself?"

Steve shook his head. "I really wouldn't suggest that as being the best way. Most lawyers have experience in drawing up wills and only charge a few hundred dollars, at the most. Plus, if you go with the lawyer, they can keep the information at their office, and have the will readily available when you die. A homemade will is better than no will, but I'd suggest you use a lawyer to increase your chances of having the will executed smoothly.

"Each will needs to name an executor. In addition to distributing to the beneficiaries their share of the assets, the executor handles the payment of all debts and collects all money owed to the estate. So it's always good defense to have a list on hand of whom you owe, and, more importantly, who owes you. You should get someone you trust to be the executor, and make sure they'll agree to the job before assigning them the responsibility."

"Are we allowed to change our will?" Pete asked.

"Like everything else we've talked about, a will should be reviewed regularly. I would suggest reviewing the will every three years. It needs to be modified, in particular, if you have dependants that are not mentioned in your current will, or if you've changed your mind about how you want your assets to be distributed. The most important thing, though, is to have a will written down and signed by two witnesses (neither of whom are beneficiaries).

"Another strategy to defend against unexpected events is to have insurance. Accidents happen, and it is easier to budget a little a month than to have one huge expense when you least expect it. There are three major kinds of insurance most people get: car insurance, homeowner/tenant insurance and life insurance. The first two are fairly similar, so we'll look at them first.

"The whole strategy for buying home insurance and car insurance is to avoid large expenses. They each have their own idiosyncrasies. First, let's look at car insurance, since Chris won't need tenant's insurance for a while. There are several parts to car insurance. Costs incurred with car insurance include liability (damage inflicted on others and their property) and collision (damage inflicted on your own car). To defend against large expenses, make sure you take liability insurance. Even the best drivers experience poor weather conditions, and lawsuits for damage to others and their property can be very expensive. Better safe than sorry. Collision insurance is great when your car is new or nearly new. As it starts getting older, you have to decide if the insurance is worth it. Certainly don't spend four hundred dollars per year for a car worth five hundred dollars.

"Tenant or homeowner insurance (depending on whether you rent or own your residence) protects your property from damage or loss due to fire, theft or other circumstances. Make sure you check the policy for which actual 'circumstances' they cover. Most standard policies will cover water damage, but will not cover 'Acts of God' like earthquakes, lightning strikes and cyclones.

"When purchasing tenant or homeowner insurance, make sure you get the replacement value on the insured items. Having the depreciated value is not worth the insurance. If you have a $4,000 furniture set which is lost or damaged, the depreciated value may only be $1,000. Meanwhile, you need new furniture. So make sure your insurance covers the replacement value. Like car insurance, homeowner insurance usually includes provision for liability (or damage inflicted on others)."

"Insurance seems kind of expensive," Pete observed. "Are there any ways to save money on it?"

"One of the things you can do," Steve offered, "is to get a higher deductible. This is the amount which is deducted from your damages, and which you'll have to pay when damages are incurred. Since you're using the insurance to defend yourself against large losses, determine what you'd consider to be an acceptable deductible – like $300, $500 or $1,000. Ask your insurance agent how much you'd save on your premiums (that is, your annual payments) if you increased your deductible – it can become quite significant.

"Another thing you can do is to pay for the full year in one lump sum. If you pay monthly premiums, you're usually charged interest and/or administration fees. So check out that option to reduce the amount you pay for insurance.

"Whereas insurance on your car and residence is defense against large expenses, life insurance is defense against both large expenses and loss of income. Life insurance typically covers the expenses of paying for the funeral, paying off your outstanding debts, and paying estate taxes due upon your death. This eases the financial strain on the surviving family members.

"The main purpose of life insurance, though, is usually to protect the surviving family members from the loss of income they are dependent on. Life insurance is especially important for couples who have one spouse earning much more money than the other spouse. If the higher-wage earner were to die, the lower-wage earner would be left with the task of meeting his or her retirement goals without the expected assistance of the former spouse's wages. If the lower-wage earner were to die first, the spouse would still need insurance, but the coverage would not have to be as high."

"Again," Pete added, "I've got to say that insurance can be expensive. Have you got any tips for keeping the price of life insurance down?"

"Once you've determined," Steve responded, "how much life insurance you'll need to cover your expenses and loss of income, you can do a number of things to save money. You should shop around and get at least three quotes for your insurance.

"Often people get life insurance on their mortgages. When the mortgages are insured, the value of the mortgage decreases while the premium stays the same. That is, you pay the same amount each month while your future payout decreases. The mortgage holder is often a bank, and they tend to charge more to insure you than a standard life insurance company would. So check around before signing on the dotted line.

"If you're younger than fifty, and are in good health, shop for term life insurance, not the whole life insurance. With term life, you'll pay lower premiums for a certain term, often five or ten years. Then the premiums will increase as you age. Even though the premiums are increasing, you'll be dollars ahead by sticking with term life insurance. Just be careful that your needs are being met. In a ten-year term, your income may vary significantly. If you want to change the coverage (that is, the payout upon death), you'll probably have to pay a penalty. But often it's worth the penalty if you experience large salary increases.

Pete asked, "Should I be getting life insurance for my children?"

Steve replied, "You could get a small policy to cover their funeral. But you don't really need much more than that in normal circumstances.

"And that covers everything I wanted to say about defense against unexpected events. Make sure you have a will, car insurance, tenant/homeowner insurance and life insurance which meet your needs.

"The last opponent you'll want to defend yourself against is investment losses. First off, let me say that if you've got your money in mutual funds, then you should expect losses over the short term while gaining over the long term. Your major strategies should be to buy and hold, and to diversify your holdings. But if your fund is heavy in a certain niche, like technology, then you must keep your eyes on that niche sector. Follow what the experts in the niche are saying, and if the future doesn't look bright, get your money out of that niche. Do not, however, pull your money out of stocks every time the prices go down. Instead, continue to buy on the dollar cost averaging basis (which I'll be speaking about next week). History has shown us that a bear market (marked by decreasing values in the major stock indices) is always followed by a bull market (marked by increasing values in the major stock indices). It can actually be a good time to buy stocks when their prices go down.

"If your money is in long-term bonds (which I'll talk more about next week), you have to watch interest rates. If you expect interest rates to increase, then you can expect bond returns to decrease. So avoid buying bonds in the short term if interest rates are on the rise.

"If you invest in stocks, then you can ask your stockbroker for a stop-loss order to defend yourself against huge losses. That is, you can instruct your broker to sell the stock if the price drops below whatever loss you're willing to tolerate. For instance, if you buy a stock at $20, and are willing to tolerate a loss of 25 percent, then you can instruct your stockbroker to sell if the price of the stock drops below $15. A stop-loss order usually has a time limit of thirty days. So watch out for any time limits.

"Just to review the week," Steve wrapped up, "there are a number of things you need to do to defend your savings. You need to defend yourself against overspending, high-interest debt, unfair taxes, inflation, unexpected events and investment losses. Does anyone have any questions?"

"Do we get to cover offense next week?" Pete begged.

"Yes," Steve replied. "Next week we'll work on going on the offense – and I'll help you work on increasing your earnings."

Jenny chuckled, "Pete, you've always called my Dad a cheapskate. After tonight, I think it's more appropriate to call him 'an excellent defender of his savings.'" The gang chuckled as Steve handed out the week's review sheets.

Set Up a Good Defense

Defense against overspending
- Spend less than you earn through proper budgeting.
- Shop around.
- Maintain your house and car.

Defense against high interest debt
- Avoid debt as much as possible.
- Lower interest rates on the debt you have.

Defense against unfair taxes
- Keep good records.

Defense against inflation
- Choose investments that beat inflation.

Defense against unexpected events
- Wills
- Car insurance
- Tenant/homeowner insurance
- Life insurance

Defense against investment losses
- Diversify holdings.
- Use buy and hold long-term strategy.
- Use stop-loss orders with stocks.

Practice Session 5
Gear Up Your Offense

The students were seated and ready to go when Steve showed up the usual ten minutes early. "Look at the eager beavers!" Steve commented.

Pete quipped, "I've waited five weeks to find out how to make more money. You're darn right I'm eager!"

Steve began, "I mentioned last week that you can increase your savings by either spending less money, earning more money, or both. Tonight we'll talk about strategies to make more money, or, as I like to call it, 'gearing up the offense.' Just as in hockey, there are several offensive strategies to make more money, and several variations on each strategy. The four main strategies for making money are the earnings offense, the financial assets offense, the real estate offense and the business offense. Let's discuss how each offense works.

"The first offensive strategy is to increase your earned income. Earned income is money made by working for others in a relationship where work is done for a certain amount of money. Any money you make on a job is considered earned income. When you get paid on a salary (typically on a per-hour or per-annum basis), the money you make is earned by performing certain tasks. If you're working in a job where you get paid by the hour, the two most obvious ways to increase your income are to increase the hours you work or to increase the rate of pay that you get per hour. To increase the hours you work, you could either offer to work more at your current job, or you could find a part-time job. The first week I spoke to the group of you, we discussed what type of players you are. Ideally, find a part-time job that lets you follow your passion and/or a job that lets you use your strengths.

"To increase the rate you're getting paid, there are a few things you can do. The main thing you should concentrate on is how to add value to your current occupation. Ask your supervisor what you could do to increase your salary. You might want to get more training. Take a night course or two in a subject related to your current occupation.

"You could also look at moving up the employment ladder. Find out how the people you work for got their jobs, and follow their path. Also, speak with others who have a career you may be interested in, and find out what they did to get to where they are. It's important that you are enthusiastic about your occupation if you want to make more money. I spoke the first week about where your skills and interests are. Do they match your current occupation?

"I also spoke the first week about becoming an expert in your field. The expert in any field is usually the highest paid employee. Look at the best hockey players in the world as an example. Becoming an expert, though, takes time, commitment and sacrifice. Ask yourself what area is important enough to you that you are willing to commit yourself to it and spend the time needed to become the best in your field. Once you've decided on which expertise you'd like to pursue, make it your goal to become the expert in that field. Nowadays, with a global economy, you can have an expertise in a very narrow field, and still make a good living.

"Another possible route to making more money in your current occupation is offering to do your work on a consulting basis. As work becomes more project-driven, it's feasible that more people will be hired only as long as the project lasts. Mark does consulting, and can testify to the fact that self-employment makes it easier to defend yourself against taxes because you can decide where the money you're paid will go, and you can claim some tax deductions which employed people may not be entitled to. Another advantage of self-employment is that you can usually charge more money on an hourly basis than you would earn as an employee. Other advantages are that you've got more variety in your tasks. You get to be involved in sales, marketing and finance in addition to your occupation."

Pete asked, "With all due respect to Mark, who wants the headaches of worrying about all that other stuff?"

Steve replied, "Many people are attracted to the extra income opportunities, while others are more or less forced into the situation when they're laid off from their company, and then offered back the same job on a consulting basis. Outsourcing is becoming very popular, so expect self-employed consultants to increase in numbers.

"To increase your earned income, then, you could either work more hours, move up the ladder, become an expert, become self-employed, or a combination of all these things. The important thing to do is to find a job that lets you demonstrate your strengths and pursue your interests."

"But Steve," Pete interjected, " this is the route I've been taking. I want to free up some time so I can play street hockey with the kids. How can we make more money without working ourselves to death?"

"Great question!" Steve responded. "The next offensive strategy is to create or increase your financial assets. With financial assets, you want to get the money you have working for you. To do this, your three major players are time, rate of return and principal. If you can increase any of these, then your money will make even more money.

"Two weeks ago, we looked at an example of how time affects our investments. If you get the money in earlier, savings can grow longer, and hence get much bigger.

"Increasing the rate of return on your investments in financial assets can also have a big effect on the money you have. Let's look at how an investment of $1,000 can grow over the next 25 years at different rates of return."

	Rate of Return			
	5%	10%	15%	20%
0	$1,000.00	$1,000.00	$1,000.00	$1,000.00
1	$1,050.00	$1,100.00	$1,150.00	$1,200.00
2	$1,102.50	$1,210.00	$1,322.50	$1,440.00
3	$1,157.63	$1,331.00	$1,520.88	$1,728.00
4	$1,215.51	$1,464.10	$1,749.01	$2,073.60
5	$1,276.28	$1,610.51	$2,011.36	$2,488.32
6	$1,340.10	$1,771.56	$2,313.06	$2,985.98
7	$1,407.10	$1,948.72	$2,660.02	$3,583.18
8	$1,477.46	$2,143.59	$3,059.02	$4,299.82
9	$1,551.33	$2,357.95	$3,517.88	$5,159.78
10	$1,628.89	$2,593.74	$4,045.56	$6,191.74
11	$1,710.34	$2,853.12	$4,652.39	$7,430.08
12	$1,795.86	$3,138.43	$5,350.25	$8,916.10
13	$1,885.65	$3,452.27	$6,152.79	$10,699.32
14	$1,979.93	$3,797.50	$7,075.71	$12,839.18
15	$2,078.93	$4,177.25	$8,137.06	$15,407.02
16	$2,182.87	$4,594.97	$9,357.62	$18,488.43
17	$2,292.02	$5,054.47	$10,761.26	$22,186.11
18	$2,406.62	$5,559.92	$12,375.45	$26,623.33
19	$2,526.95	$6,115.91	$14,231.77	$31,948.00
20	$2,653.30	$6,727.50	$16,366.54	$38,337.60
21	$2,785.96	$7,400.25	$18,821.52	$46,005.12
22	$2,925.26	$8,140.27	$21,644.75	$55,206.14
23	$3,071.52	$8,954.30	$24,891.46	$66,247.37
24	$3,225.10	$9,849.73	$28,625.18	$79,496.85
25	$3,386.35	$10,834.71	$32,918.95	$95,396.22

No. of years

Growth of $1,000 over 25 Years at Different Rates of Return

Steve handed out the charts. As Mark put on his glasses, Steve continued, "In this chart, I've shown how $1,000 can grow over time at different rates of return. You'll notice that at 10 percent, $1,000 grows to $2,593.74 in the first ten years, and then jumps up to $6,727.50 after twenty years. The increase in the first ten years was $1,593.74, while the increase in the next ten years was $4,133.76! To reiterate the point I made two weeks ago, get in there as soon as you can!

"You'll also notice how an increase in the rate of return seems to more than multiply the money you're making. While a 10 percent rate of return will allow $1,000 to grow to $6,727.50 after twenty years, a 20 percent rate of return will cause the money to grow to $38,337.60 over the same time period! The rate of return is double, but the money in the account is nearly six times that of a 10 percent return.

"Similarly, the more principal you invest, the more you'll have. If you invest $3,000, for example, you can multiply all the numbers in this chart by three. When you're investing your money in financial assets, maximize the time, rate of return and principal to get the most out of your investment.

"The financial assets offense includes many different products, but today we're going to focus on some of the major ones: guaranteed return investments, bonds, stocks and mutual funds. With these products, the return on your investment goes up with the risk. The lowest risk of this set is the investments with guaranteed returns. These consist of the GIC/CD, treasury bills (T-bills) and money market funds. In the U.S., a CD is a Certificate of Deposit, while in Canada a GIC is a Guaranteed Investment Certificate. Both the CD and GIC are products you can buy from banking institutions at a certain amount for a fixed period of time. In return, they offer a guaranteed rate of return. The good news is that this money is insured up to a certain limit. Meanwhile, the federal government issues T-bills and they also offer guaranteed rates of return for locking in your money. A money market fund combines the above into a mutual fund of short-term fixed-income securities that are all maturing within the next year. While these guaranteed return investments may be useful when you know you'll need the money in a short period of time, the rates of return are usually too low for most investors to consider them for a long-term investment strategy.

"The next product you might want to consider for your offense is bonds. Bonds are sold by governments and corporations, and represent a formal IOU between you and the government or corporation issuing the bonds. With a bond, the issuer promises to pay you a certain interest rate per annum until the bond matures.

"Bonds can make you money in two ways. First, they will pay you a certain amount of interest each year. Second, bonds may be bought and sold. The value of the bond varies inversely with interest rates. That is, if interest rates go down, the value of your bond goes up. Similarly, the value of the bond will go down when interest rates go up. For instance, if you have a $1,000 bond with an interest rate of 7 percent, then you'll be getting $70 per year. If the interest rates go down to 5 percent, then your 7 percent bond is worth more money, and people will be willing to pay money to get the additional interest. So its value goes up.

"If you own bonds, you're a loaner, because you're lending money in order to get interest. When you own stocks, you are an owner. A stock is a share of a corporation. When a corporation needs money, it can either borrow the money from a bank or moneylender, or the corporation can issue shares on a publicly traded exchange. The price of the share generally increases as the corporation grows. One offensive strategy is to buy the stock when you think the stock is under-priced, and then sell the stock either when it's over-priced or when you've realized a return you're happy with."

"How do we determine if a stock is under-priced or over-priced?" Jenny asked.

"It's an excellent question to ask, but a difficult question to answer," Steve replied. "When you look up information on the price of a stock, there are several numbers given. One of the safest routes to go is to look at the P/E ratio. This refers to the Price to Earnings ratio. The price is the price per share, and the earnings are the earnings per share. When the P/E ratio is low, the stock is considered a 'value' stock. Typically, a low value is under 12, but industry averages change over time. To be considered a value stock, the share's P/E ratio needs to be less than the industry average. 'Value investors' try to buy stocks with low P/E ratios; they see the value in the high earnings and the low price.

"Another good offensive strategy is to choose stocks that offer dividends. Typically, when a company makes a profit at the end of the year, they can either re-invest the profits in the company or give the profits to the shareholders. Many companies that offer dividends choose to do both. For instance, if company XYZ has a profit of $300,000, they can keep $200,000 to re-invest (also called retained earnings), and then distribute the remaining $100,000 evenly among the shareholders. If there are 500,000 shares outstanding, each shareholder would receive an annual dividend of 20 cents ($100,000/500,000). Some companies offer dividends even when they are not making money. This may be because the company is in a cyclical industry where they expect more profits down the road, or because the company wants to remain competitive to keep its shareholders.

"Choosing a stock that offers dividends gives you extra income without having to sell the stock. The best strategy to take is to re-invest the dividends in the stock you own. This allows the investment to grow even if the stock price remains the same.

"To get higher dividends, you can choose to purchase preferred shares of a corporation (rather than common shares). With preferred shares, you usually sacrifice voting rights. Also, the value of the preferred shares is tied more to interest rates than to the growth of the company. It's a better long-term strategy to stick with common shares of growth companies than to opt for the preferred shares.

"The value of a dividend is measured by the dividend yield. The dividend yield is the dividend per share divided by the price per share, expressed as a percentage. We can look at a few examples. Company ABC could be giving a dividend of 60 cents per share, with a share price of $20. This would give a dividend yield of 3 percent. Meanwhile, company DEF could be giving a lower dividend of 50 cents per share, but its share price is only $10. Its dividend yield would be 5 percent. If we were to invest $100 in each of the two companies, we'd be getting a $3 dividend from company ABC, but we'd be getting a $5 dividend from company DEF.

"To buy stocks, you need to go through a broker, which, of course, involves a fee. Different brokers charge different fees. 'Discount brokers' charge in the range of $15-$35 for a basic transaction, and will simply process your request to buy or sell stocks. 'Full-service brokers' typically charge $65-$100 for a basic transaction. The full service they offer is that they will give you advice on what to buy and what not to buy. Some full-service brokers also like to charge an annual fee to handle your account. Often they will waive the annual fee when your investments are large, or if you belong to a specified group or company. Make sure you ask about these discounts when shopping for an investment agency to work with.

"Buying stocks can be lucrative, but it can also cause your savings to fall. Before embarking heavily on a stock purchase program, it's good to try it on paper for six to twelve months. That is, pretend you've purchased a certain amount of shares, and write down on paper how many you've purchased. Note the fluctuation in the stock price, its P/E ratio, and its dividend yield. Calculate your profit or loss by including the broker's fees and the necessary taxes."

Pete asked, "I haven't heard you mention what my brother is always telling me to get into. How do mutual funds compare with stocks, bonds and guaranteed rate investments?"

Steve replied, "Mutual funds have been a great offensive strategy to earn more income. The depth and breadth of these funds continue to grow. To follow the discussion of guaranteed return investments, bonds and stocks, I'll talk about mutual funds in the ascending order of risk and return.

"A mutual fund is a fund to which many people can contribute their money, and then the fund manager decides which money products to allocate the money to. Mutual funds come in many shapes and colors. Many investors like them because they allow a hands-off investment which is diversified. Each fund has a manager, and the manager worries about how to spend the money in the fund. While this can be a good thing, the manager doesn't come for free. The expenses involved in managing the fund are referred to as the Management Expense Ratio (MER). The MER of an equity fund typically runs in the range of 2 to 3 percent, and includes the manager's fee and operating expenses.

"Mutual funds involve risks and return rates similar to the products in their funds. The lowest-risk funds are the money market funds, which I was discussing earlier. Bond funds are funds that invest in bonds of varying lengths. The main intent of these funds is to provide income for their holders. Like normal bonds, these funds are susceptible to varying interest rates. The longer the term of the bonds, the more volatile the bonds can become. Conversely, a bond fund that invests primarily in bonds maturing in one to three years will be the most stable.

"Income funds have the express purpose of producing income. They are usually made up primarily of government and corporate bonds. These are usually very predictable, and tend to offer slightly higher rates than money market funds. These are great when you've made the decision to retire, or if you're within five years of retirement and you're on target to reach your retirement goals.

"Equity funds invest in common stocks. These funds vary widely in their holdings, and there is a large selection of funds available. Most of them fall into the following categories: small-cap, large-cap, sector and index. Cap is a short form for capitalization, and is found by multiplying the share price by the number of shares outstanding. Stocks for big companies like Wal-Mart™ and Coca-Cola™ would typically be included in a large-cap fund, while small-cap funds would include companies with a much smaller number of shares outstanding. The small-cap funds have more room to grow, and the successful small-cap funds have outperformed the large-cap funds over the last forty years.

"Sector funds are mutual funds which concentrate on a certain sector of the economy, such as technology or financial services. While they can be a good part of your offense, they require you to watch the sector carefully. Technology was hot for a while, but has now cooled down. The gold and oil sectors are now growing, but we don't know how long that will last.

"The last major type of equity mutual fund is the index fund. These have gained popularity recently because the MER is much lower than most of the equity funds. The reason for this is that the manager merely has to follow the index, rather than actively picking stocks. The problem with index funds is that they are usually outperformed in a bear market by funds managed by active fund managers.

"There are also international funds available. Fund managers will choose a certain country or region of the world to watch, and then focus on one of the above types of funds in that region. Investors can often find great value in investing in countries outside their own, since different areas of the world are experiencing different growth rates.

"Mutual funds are very convenient. You can use a monthly deduction program to purchase them. Since they are managed professionally by the fund manager, you needn't worry too much about where the money is going. To get the most out of this offense, it is best to do your homework. Look at the statistics of the different fund managers out there. Which ones have been consistently good? Speak with friends, read analysts' reports. Get a sense of which fund managers you think would give you the greatest return on your money.

"Monthly or bi-weekly deductions are a great way to purchase mutual funds. The term for this is dollar-cost averaging. This allows you to distribute your investment evenly, and reduces your risk of buying at the wrong time. Let's look at an example. In this example, our wise investor will commit to spending $120 a month on a certain fund that is considered to be a good value. The fund price may be $10 per share one month, $8 per share the next, and $12 per share the third month. Each month the investor is getting a different number of shares. The first month 12 shares will be purchased. The second month 15 shares will be purchased, and the third month 10 shares will be purchased. In this example, the investment has been $360, but the current value is $444. That's quite a return!

"This isn't magic either. It's a result of investing a fixed amount of money at regular intervals. It allows you to buy more shares when the price is low, and fewer shares when the price is high. The key here is to stay in for the long term. Don't get out just because prices drop; you'll actually be getting more stocks when this happens. When the prices rebound, which the stock market has done consistently, you'll have more shares of the fund appreciating in value.

"With mutual funds, there is not necessarily a fee every time you buy, as there is in stocks. Rather, there is a 'load' associated with mutual funds. Funds can charge either a front-end load, a back-end load or no-load. A front-end load fund means that you'll pay the commission as soon as you buy the fund. A back-end load fund requires you to pay only when you sell the fund. This commission is usually done on a degrading scale, so you'll pay less each year you keep your money in the fund. While the back-end load fund sounds better in terms of commission, the MER is typically higher than the front-end load funds. A no-load fund means there is no commission paid by the consumer, but again the MER is often higher for a no-load fund."

Pete interrupted, "Steve, the financial assets offense sounds great to me, but I don't have the time or interest to keep up on all these things. What approach should I take?"

Steve smiled. "The best long-term strategy for you, in that case, would be to investigate mutual fund managers that you'll feel comfortable giving your money to. Read their stats; that is, see how they've done in the past. Speak with investment professionals to get their advice as well. Then choose which mutual fund, or funds, you want to contribute to, and make contributions every paycheck. Discipline wins hockey games, and it also brings you more wealth. Start today, so time will be on your side as much as possible.

"Along with financial assets, the real estate offense is a very traditional strategy for making more money. There are two main strategies in this offense for building your wealth. Either you flip a property, or you buy it and hold on to it for a long time. Flipping a property consists of buying a property at below-market value, and then selling it fairly quickly at market value. Finding properties at below-market value is not always easy, but there are ways you can increase your chances. Many players in this game are either real estate agents or friends of agents, and so hear about the good deals before the normal consumer. Other flippers visit the courthouse to find out which houses are in foreclosure or are about to go into foreclosure. Some of the more successful players in this game advertise the fact that they buy houses, and attract sellers that way. There are lots of ways to play offense in this area, and a good place to start is to read *Nothing Down* by Robert G. Allen. It certainly helped me when I was starting in real estate.

"A long-term strategy with real estate is to buy houses, apartments, duplexes, et cetera and then rent them out while you wait for their value to increase. As the rents increase over the years, you'll realize more and more passive income as the mortgage remains constant. For example, you might purchase a property with a monthly mortgage payment of $600 for five years. The rent may be $625 per month the first year, then go up to $640 per month the next year. By the time the fifth year arrives, the rent could be up to $700 per month. Each year, your income is increasing since the rent is going up, but the mortgage payment is staying constant.

"In addition to the rental income, a significant gain can be made as the value of the house appreciates. Since the tenant is effectively paying the mortgage for you, you can make a good deal of money by holding on to a house for a long time, and then selling it."

"Hasn't real estate run its course?" Mark wondered.

"Real estate prices continue to rise, especially when the stock market doesn't perform well, or when interest rates fall. Look at what people were paying for houses in this neighborhood 15 years ago, and compare that with what they're paying for them now. Project those numbers forward another 15 years, and you'll see the income you're capable of adding to your retirement funds. The best news is that the tenants pay off the mortgage."

"Steve," Mark interrupted, "the return is not that great. The houses around here have doubled in price in the last 15 years. If I'm getting a 10 percent return on my mutual funds, then they'll double in just over seven years. In 15 years, my money's going to quadruple."

"Interesting point, Mark," Steve surmised, "but the return on your real estate investment is much greater than a hundred percent. Traditionally, you would only put down 25 percent. So if you can get the house price to double in the same time it takes to pay off the mortgage, then your investment is worth eight times the initial down payment! Remember when looking at real estate that your investment is often just the down payment. If you do apply a larger down payment, then your rental income will be larger.

"The last offensive strategy I want to discuss with you tonight is starting your own business. Assuming you follow standard business practices, you can use a business to significantly increase your financial position. As an employee of the business, you can give yourself a salary. By controlling the finances around the business, you can determine the best way to defend yourself and your business against overspending on taxes. The government has instituted many laws to help small business owners with their tax deductions since they know some small businesses will evolve into big businesses (and big businesses pay lots of taxes).

"In addition to earned income, a business can give you investment income as a result of the business itself becoming more valuable as it grows. The trick to making investment income from your business is to have a set of systems and procedures that make it easy for someone else to take over the business once you're ready to sell it. McDonald's is a great example. They have a set of procedures for choosing a location to build a restaurant. They also have procedures for serving customers, and for making their products. They combine that with marketing systems and training systems to offer a business which people want to buy into. Too many business owners get tied up with doing the actual work that they miss the opportunity to sell the business when they are finished with it. Avoid that pitfall.

"A business will also give you the opportunity to make passive income. You can set up a dividend program to pay yourself profits from the business each year. Also, if you set up people to do all the work for you, you can go sit on the sidelines and let others do the work while you get paid. This will give you more time to work on the systems so that the business can become more valuable. When an offer comes along, you can decide if it's better to sell the business or to continue with the passive income being generated.

"While a business offers the best offense, it also has the most risk. Eighty percent of businesses fail in the first five years. Also, to get the business up and running takes a lot of time and commitment. You need to stay energetic and enthusiastic about what you're doing to keep the business alive. If you do decide to start a business, make sure it's in line with where you see your strengths and your interests. Figure out what type of player you are, and then try to build a business around that. Think back to your answers to the questionnaires that I gave you a few weeks ago.

"You could drop everything you're doing, and start a business tomorrow. But a more prudent thing, and a way to increase your chances of success, is to start in your spare time. Think about the value you can offer customers, and choose a group of customers that you would like to serve. Find out what that group, called a target market, needs and what they are willing to pay for. I've seen too many engineering firms that first make a product, and then try to find a market for that product. Your chance of success is much better if you select the market, find out what they want, and then give it to them. This makes more business sense. Then make a business plan, get it reviewed, and implement it!"

"I'm pretty well finished describing all the offensive strategies you need to get started. Just to review, you could make more money in what you do now, you could find a higher-paying job, or you could find a part-time job to supplement your earned income. You could also start contributing money to financial assets to get your money working for you. The best strategy with the least amount of effort is to set up a contribution from each paycheck to be used to purchase mutual funds. You could also make more money by getting into real estate. This would involve either flipping properties in a short time period, or renting out properties to give you rental income while the mortgage is being paid off. The last offensive strategy I've given you is to start your own business. Choose something you are interested in. Plan the work, and then work the plan."

Pete spoke up, "I want to get the last word tonight, because Jenny has had more than her fair share of finishing the conversation each time. I'm going to use more than one offensive strategy to get more money in my savings. I want my money to work for me."

Jenny said, "That makes sense, Pete."

Pete shot back, "What does, dear?"

Jenny mused, "We're a one-income family living in a world designed for families making two incomes. By adding offensive strategies, we're adding more incomes. How would they say that in hockey? We've got more players shooting on the net."

Once again, Jenny had had the last word. Pete and the gang collected the review sheets from Steve as he headed out the door. Pete posted his on his blackboard, and took a long hard look at it.

Gear Up Your Offense

Earned income
- Become an expert in a field that matches your strengths and interests.
- Get a part-time job to supplement your income.

Financial assets
- Maximize time, rate of return and principal.
- Put your savings into guaranteed investments, bonds, stocks, mutual funds.

Real estate
- Flip properties quickly for profit.
- Collect rents from real estate holdings.

Mind your own business
- Investigate a business that matches your strengths and interests.
- Start in your spare time, and set up systems so the business can eventually be sold.

Practice Session 6
Keep on Top of the Game

Steve opened with, "You must be happy the offense has been covered now, Pete?"

Pete smiled. "It sure is good to have so many fresh ideas on how to make money. You've covered how to save, and how to earn. What else is there?"

Steve responded, "I've mentioned several times how things change. Tax laws change. Rates of inflation change. Your return on investment in the stock market and in real estate changes. To handle all these changes takes energy. I've given you some tools, like the $HM book, to help you improve your finances. I've told you about other tools, like a retirement calculator. But the biggest and most important tool in managing your money is YOU. While everything is changing, your brain has to react and decide which path to take next. To keep your brain in good working shape, and to keep your energy levels high, there are a few things you need to do to stay on top of your game.

"You have to stay fit in four different areas: your body, your mind, your spirit and your interaction with others. First, there's physical fitness. North Americans are not very fit. In Canada, 63 percent of us are over-weight, while in the U.S., over 30 percent of children are considered obese. Being overweight increases the chances of heart problems and type 2 diabetes. Also, being overweight causes a drain on our energy levels as we lug around the extra weight, and expend more energy eating."

"I'm not overweight," Jenny said, "but I'm certainly far from fit."

"Good point, Jenny," Steve replied. "Since this lesson is about fitness, let's concentrate on that. Physical fitness requires two things to reach your optimal level: eating well and exercising regularly. Eating well means several things. Raw fruits and vegetables are much healthier, and will give you much more energy, than most fatty foods. The government often publishes guidelines on what constitutes a healthy balance. In addition to plenty of fruits and vegetables, a balanced eating plan will also include dairy products, meat products or meat substitutes, and breads and cereals. Follow a balanced eating plan, and your energy level will rise. Just make sure you don't overeat.

"The second part of physical fitness is regular exercise. Whether you like to swim, run, bike, roller-blade or play street hockey, you need to exercise at least three times per week. Each time you exercise, you should make sure your heart is at an elevated rate for at least twenty minutes each time. Being physically fit will give you more energy to pursue your goals – and, of course, will make you a better street hockey player.

"In addition to being physically fit, intellectual fitness is important to stay ahead in the personal finance game. With the Internet, there are libraries upon libraries of information at our fingertips. We have access to more information than ever before. Often, all this information can be overwhelming. Whether you want to figure out ways to reach your financial goals, or whether you want to look at maximizing your income potential by starting your own business, your brain has to be in shape to determine all the possibilities, and to decide on the best plan of action. Look at it this way: if you read one book per month on a certain topic, you could easily become an expert in that area in less than four years.

"Many of us think that when the schooling ends, so does our education. As we mature, we realize that nothing could be further from the truth. Commit yourself to becoming a lifelong learner. Get information from books, television, newspapers, magazines and the Internet. Both you and the world will be richer for it.

"The body and mind can work together with our spirit to move us towards our goals. The next element of fitness is what I refer to as emotional fitness, and it encompasses handling your emotions and feeding your spirit. To enjoy a well-balanced life, you need to get in touch with your feelings, both good and bad. Good feelings, such as happiness and fulfillment, can be recognized and amplified. If the methods you use to earn your income are making you feel good inside, you will be drawn to do a better job, which in turn will help you make more money. I've said it before but it's worth repeating: you need a job that will let you demonstrate your strengths and pursue your interests. Having a job that does not feed your good feelings will either have no effect, or it will feed the bad feelings.

"Another thing you can do to stay emotionally fit is to monitor your behavior when you recognize bad feelings, such as fear and anger. Such feelings are a necessary part of life, but how you respond to those feelings is something you can work on. The next time you recognize fear or anger, determine how this came to be. Could you avoid the situation in the future? And how did you react? Could you react differently in a similar future situation?

"The spirit, like the mind and the body, needs to be fed. Each week, reward yourself for the accomplishments you've made. Whether it's a chocolate or a walk on the beach, you'll feel better when you recognize your own accomplishments. Accentuating the positive is a good way to live, and encourages positive energy to flow.

"Being in harmony with yourself is a good way to keep your energy levels high. But to reach the big goals in your life, including most of the financial goals, you will need the help of others. The last element of my energy program is to maintain your social fitness. Social fitness entails communicating with others. There are two main elements to be fit in this area. In addition to being able to speak well, you also need to be a good listener. If you join a group like Toastmasters, you will be able to improve in both these areas.

"Becoming a more effective speaker or conversationalist requires certain skills which are learned by giving speeches and holding conversations. Preferably, these conversations will be held with others who don't hold the same opinions as you. Listening skills can be learned from practicing as well, but lots of good conversationalists have problems developing their listening skills. Many teachers of listening skills say the number one obstacle that people experience to becoming better listeners is that they simply don't care what the other person is saying. People want to be heard, but do not necessarily want to hear. To become socially fit, you need to become both an effective speaker and an effective listener. If you want to be heard, it's only reasonable that you should grant the person you're speaking with the same consideration.

"Becoming a better listener will help you in reaching your goals. If you're able to determine both what the bank manager (or your financial advisor, or even your spouse) is saying to you, and why she's saying it, you will be able to create a much better bond with that person. I mentioned during our 'scoring your goals' session that having a great team around you will increase your chances of success. Being able to both express your feelings and understand what your team members are saying will allow optimum teamwork to be achieved. Social fitness is very important in reaching your financial goals.

"The good thing about the four elements of fitness is that they feed each other. A healthy body helps the brain function properly. A well-exercised brain can come up with methods of meeting your emotional needs. When you're feeling good, others want to communicate with you, and you care what they have to say.

"Together, these four elements of fitness provide a very strong foundation for whichever endeavor you choose to pursue. Whether you want to get rid of your debt, like Pete and Jenny, or start on a lifelong savings program, like Chris, do your best to stay fit in each of these areas."

"Hmmm," Jenny pondered.

Mark said, "Here we go again. Jenny's always got to get the last word in before Steve posts his review. What is it this time, sis?"

Jenny smiled, "I was just thinking of the four elements of fitness and how they're going to help me improve my energy levels. Looking at the first letter of the four elements (Physical, Intellectual, Emotional, Social) gives me a great idea on how to remember this program . . . Get Fit from PIES!"

As the band dispersed for the night, Steve handed out the review forms and Pete tacked his up on the bulletin board for one last review.

Stay on Top of Your Game

Physical fitness

- Eat well-balanced meals.
- Exercise at least three times a week.

Intellectual fitness

- Learn from books, television, magazines, Internet, etc.
- Become a lifelong learner.

Emotional fitness

- Handle your emotions.
- Feed your spirit.

Social fitness

- Speak well.
- Listen well.

Game On

Put the Puck in the Net

Pete welcomed Steve in. "Here we are. Lucky week number seven. Wasn't that your number in cage hockey, Steve?"

Steve replied, "I was a big fan of Phil Esposito. He could do no wrong in my book."

Mark and Chris walked in for the final lesson. Everyone took a seat as Steve began the last session.

"We've discussed over the last six weeks some strategies to improve your financial situation. Tonight, I want to review these strategies, and give you one last push to help you achieve what you want in your lives.

"In the first week, I spoke about determining what type of player you are. You need to discover what it is that will drive you to change your current financial habits. In order to achieve your highest form of success, you should align the work you do with your strengths and interests. Everybody's definition of financial success is different. So everybody has to individualize his or her own plan to achieve the success in finances that he or she is looking for. Examine your strengths, your interests and your priorities.

"In week two, I spoke about methods to help you score your goals. You need to write them down on a scorecard, and review them regularly. Dreams add color to our lives, and having goals helps us live those dreams. The goals, though, need game plans. Breaking the goal down into baby steps allows us to keep moving forward as the baby steps are achieved. Remember that a marathon starts with one step forward.

"Hopefully, you've all got big goals. To reach those goals requires the help, guidance and support of others. So gather a dream team to help you score those goals. Also look at the wet tennis balls, or obstacles, which are keeping you from reaching those goals. Determine ways to get around them. When the goal is written down, the game plan is ready, the team is assembled and the obstacles are outlined, it's time to drop the puck and start moving towards that goal.

"In our third week, I explained how you need to be involved for the whole sixty minutes. Success in investing comes from using time and rates of return to get your money working for you. Get involved early. In addition to allowing the compound interest to grow, early involvement also boosts your investment knowledge and allows you to get started with the right habits. Keep good financial habits through the whole sixty minutes. Pay yourself first. Save money directly from your paycheck before you get a chance to spend it. Also, monitor your spending and follow a monthly budget. Don't forget to give some money to charity as well. Prepare for the end game. Don't get caught in retirement with no savings. Put away the necessary money while you're working so you can enjoy your retirement years.

"Week number four introduced you to defense. While lots of money will flow through your hands, it's important to defend your savings before they are lost to overspending. Shop around before you buy. Don't go over budget, and avoid debt. If you find yourself with debt, reduce the interest rate as much as possible. Defend yourself against inflation by investing your savings in vehicles that beat inflation after taxes. Defend yourself against unexpected events by writing a will, and by purchasing car, home and life insurance. Defend yourself against investment losses by keeping your head up and watching those investments. If you're investing in stocks, put a stop-loss order in with the stockbroker to avoid unacceptable losses as much as possible.

"Pete was excited when we moved to the offense in week five. We discussed the four main strategies of increasing the money you make: earned income offense, financial assets offense, real estate offense and the business offense. You can increase your earned income by working more hours or by increasing the rate you get paid per hour. Your financial assets offense includes guaranteed rate investments, bonds, stocks and mutual funds. Maximizing your investments in time, rates of return and principal can create more wealth with this offense. The real estate offense can help you create more money by either flipping a property or using a buy-and-hold strategy. Flipping involves buying at wholesale and selling at retail in a short period of time. A buy-and-hold strategy lets you collect rental income while the house appreciates in price. Having a business is another great offensive strategy to make more money. Although it's risky, a business can be both financially and spiritually rewarding, especially if you find a business that matches your skills and interests.

"Last week, we discussed how you can stay on top of your game. To create a solid foundation, and to keep your energy levels high, you should stay fit physically, intellectually, emotionally and socially. In addition to good financial habits, it's important to develop good lifestyle habits to maintain your fitness in each of those categories.

"I know that not everybody wants to be a street hockey millionaire. Some people want to be financially stable so they can sleep at night. Some people want to have more time with their ailing parents. Some people want to leave a legacy behind so others can enjoy their money. Whatever reason you have for wanting to improve your financial situation, I feel confident that you now have several tools to go out and do just that. Determine who you are and where you want to be. Then determine how much money it will take to get there. Follow the methods I've shared with you to score the goals. Set up your defense, and then gear up your offense. Keep your energy levels high, and keep your enthusiasm flowing!"

With that, Steve pulled out a box of hockey sweaters. Each had "Street Hockey Millionaire" written on the front, with individual names printed on the back. The last sweater Steve pulled out was Pete's. Pete was so happy, and so highly motivated, that he couldn't resist doing something he hadn't done in thirty years. He gave Steve a big hug and said, "Thank you."

Not wanting to break tradition, the Street Hockey Millionaires let Jenny have the last word. She looked into everyone's eyes and said, "Come on, team! Let's go put those bucks in the net!"

Please visit
www.streethockeymillionaire.com
for more information.

Recommended Reading

Allen, Robert and Hansen, Mark Victor. *One Minute Millionaire.* Harmony Books, New York City, 2002.

Kiyosaki, Robert. *Rich Dad, Poor Dad.* Warner Books, New York City, 1998.

Chilton, David. *The Wealthy Barber.* Toronto, 1989.

Whyte, Jennifer. *Work Less, Make More.* John Wiley & Sons, New York City, 1999.

Waschka, Larry and McDougall, Bruce. *The Complete Idiot's Guide to Getting Rich in Canada.* Prentice Hall Canada, Scarborough, Ontario, 1998.

McFeat, Tom, Heady, Robert K. And Heady, Christy. *The Complete Idiot's Guide to Managing Your Money in Canada.* Prentice Hall Canada, Toronto, 2000.

Hall, Tom. *Jump Start Your Business Brain.* Brain Brew Books, Cincinnatti, Ohio, 2001.

Canfield, Jack, Hansen, Mark Victor and Hewitt, Les. *The Power of Focus.* Health Communications, Inc., Deerfield Beach, Florida, 2000.

Sher, Barbara. *Live The Life You Love.* Dell Trade Paperback, New York City, 1996.

Covey, Stephen. *The Seven Habits of Highly Effective People.* Fireside, New York City, 1989.

Diamond, Harvey and Diamond, Marilyn. *Fit For Life.* Warner Books, New York City, 1985.

Barnhart, Tod. *Financial Independence Tactics Manual.* The People's Network, Irving, Texas, 1995.

Allen, Robert. *Nothing Down For the 90s.* Simon and Schuster, New York City, 1990.

Encourage Others To Take Control of Their Financial Future

Street Hockey Millionaire can be the perfect gift for new graduates, newlyweds or anyone else who is seeking fun and simple ways to take control of their financial future.

Clip out this coupon and mail to:

Power Play Publishing
876 Stanstead Road
Ottawa, ON   CANADA
K1V 6Y5
(613) 733-3729

Or check us out on the web at:
www.streethockeymillionaire.com

Please send me _____ copies of *Street Hockey Millionaire*. I am enclosing a check or money order (not cash) for $14.95 US/$21.35 Cdn.* plus $2.50 per book for shipping and handling charges.**

Name _____

Address _____

City _____ State/Province _____

Country (if outside US/Canada) _____

Zip/Postal Code: _____

* Canadian price includes 7% for GST.
** For orders outside North America, please add $5 per book for shipping and handling charges.

STREET
HOCKEY
MILLIONAIRE

James Allan

COMMON SENSE STRATEGIES
TO WIN THE MONEY GAME

ISBN 0-9733345-0-9

National Library of Canada Cataloguing in Publication

Allan, James, 1963-
    Street hockey millionaire : common sense strategies to win
the money game / James Allan ; editor, Janet Shorten. — 1st ed.

Includes bibliographical references.
ISBN 0-9733345-0-9

    1. Finance, Personal. I. Shorten, Janet II. Title.

HG179.A447 2003   332.024'01   C2003-905352-0